AMAZING NO-BAKE CHEESECAKES COOKBOOK

100 Mouthwatering No-Bake Cheesecake Recipes for Dessert Lovers, with Tips and Techniques to Elevate Your Cheesecake Game and Impress Your Guests

Dorothy Lewis

Copyright Material ©2023

All Rights Reserved

No part of this book may be used or transmitted in any form or by any means without the proper written consent of the publisher and copyright owner, except for brief quotations used in a review. This book should not be considered a substitute for medical, legal, or other professional advice.

TABLE OF CONTENTS

TABLE OF CONTENTS 3
INTRODUCTION 7
FLORAL CHEESECAKES 8
    1. No-Bake Rose Cheesecake 9
    2. No-Bake Hibiscus Cheesecakes 11
    3. No-Bake Edible Flower Mini Cheesecakes 14
    4. No-Bake Butterfly Pea Cheesecake 17
    5. No-Bake Blueberry Lavender Cheesecake 20
    6. No-Bake Jasmine Cheesecake 23
FRUIT CHEESECAKES 25
    7. No-Bake Raspberry Lemon Cheesecake 26
    8. No-Bake Lime Cheesecake 29
    9. No-Bake Triple Berry Cheesecake 32
    10. No-Bake Blackberry Chocolate Cheesecake Cups 34
    11. No-Bake Apricot cheesecake 36
    12. No-Bake Strawberry Cheesecake 38
    13. No-Bake blueberry cheesecake 40
    14. No-Bake Apple cheesecake 42
    15. No-Bake Mango cheesecake 44
    16. No Bake Banana Cream Cheesecake 46
    17. No-Bake Vegan Berry cheesecake 49
    18. No-Bake Raspberry Cheesecake Truffles 51
    19. No-Bake Banana Oreo Cheesecake 53
    20. No-Bake Passionfruit Cheesecake 56
NUT CHEESECAKES 59
    21. No-Bake Orange and macadamia cheesecake 60
    22. No-Bake Almond Cheesecake 63

23. No-Bake chocolate hazelnut cheesecake 65
24. No-Bake Almond & Blueberry Cheesecake 67
25. No-Bake Almond Meal Cheesecake 69

VEGGIE CHEESECAKES 73
26. No-Bake Ube Cheesecake 74
27. No-Bake Pumpkin Pie Cheesecake 77
28. No-Bake Cheesecake with avocado and lime 79
29. No-Bake Gingersnap Pumpkin Cheesecake 82
30. No-Bake Pumpkin Pie Cheesecake Tart 84

HERBED CHEESECAKES 86
31. No-Bake Basil, lime, and strawberry cheesecake 87
32. No-Bake Matcha cheesecake 90
33. No-Bake Sweet Basil & Lemon Cheesecake 92
34. No-Bake Mint cheesecake 95
35. No-Bake Rosemary Honey Cheesecake 98
36. No-Bake Mint Nectarine Cheesecake Tart 101
37. No-Bake Ginger and Coriander Cheesecake 104

COOKIE AND CANDY CHEESECAKES 107
38. No-Bake Toblerone cheesecake 108
39. No-Bake Cookie Crumble Cheesecake 110
40. No-Bake Oreo Cheesecake 112
41. No-Bake Funfetti Oreo Birthday Cake Cheesecake 114
42. No-Bake Coconut macaroon cheesecake 117
43. No-Bake Choc Chip Cannoli Cheesecake 119
44. No-Bake Double Chocolate Cheesecake 121
45. No-Bake Mocha Cheesecake 125
46. No-Bake Peanut Butter Cheesecake Bombs 128

BOOZY CHEESECAKES 130
47. No-Bake Rum eggnog cheesecake 131

48. No Bake Margarita Cheesecake 134

49. No-Bake Pina colada cheesecake 136

50. No-Bake Vodka Toffee apple Cheesecake 138

BAKED CHEESECAKES 141

51. Strawberry Cheesecake French Toast 142

52. Blueberry lemon cheesecake oats 144

53. Strawberry cheesecake pancakes 146

54. Frozen fig cheesecake 148

55. Vegan Berry cheesecake 151

56. Mango cheesecake 153

57. Blueberry Cheesecake 155

58. Cranberry orange cheesecake 158

59. Lemond Rind cheesecake 160

60. Upside-down pineapple cheesecakes 162

61. Tangerine cheesecake 165

62. Walnut Cheesecake 167

63. Macadamia & lime weed cake 169

64. Blueberry Cheesecake 172

65. Gluten-Free Almond Meal Cheesecake 174

66. Fluffy Japanese Cheesecake 178

67. Double Chocolate Fudge Cheesecake 180

68. Japanese cheesecake 183

69. Pumpkin Cheesecake 185

70. Pumpkin Patch Cheesecake 187

71. Pumpkin Pie Cheesecake Bowls 189

72. Mini Monster Cheesecakes 192

73. Individual Key Lime Cheesecakes 194

74. Cardboard Box Oven Cheesecake 197

75. Low-Carb key lime cheesecakes 199

76. Cottage cheese Cheesecake ... 202
77. No-bake pumpkin crust Cheesecake ... 204
78. No bake mixed berry yuzu Cheesecake ... 206
79. Cheesecake Cupcakes ... 209
80. Custard Cup Cheesecake cupcakes ... 211
81. Cheesecake Bars ... 213
82. Pumpkin Cheesecake Bars ... 215
83. Frozen Chocolate Peanut Butter Cheesecake Bombs ... 217
84. Raspberry Cheesecake Truffles ... 219
85. Cookies & Cream Cheesecake Bites ... 221
86. Air Fryer Cheesecake Bites ... 223
87. Pumpkin pie cheesecake Tart ... 225
88. Amaretto cheesecake tarts ... 227
89. Cheesecake ice cream ... 229
90. Cheesecake Sherbet ... 231
91. Cheesecake Ice Cream Recipe ... 233
92. Blueberry Cheesecake Ice Cream ... 235
93. Apple-Cheese Ice Cream ... 238
94. Cherry Cheesecake Ice Cream ... 240
95. Smoked salmon Cheesecake ... 242
96. Chicken-chili cheesecake ... 244
97. Crab meat cheesecakes with crab ... 246
98. Daiquiri cheesecake ... 249
99. Pina colada cheesecake ... 251
100. Kahlua and cream cheesecake ... 253

CONCLUSION ... 255

INTRODUCTION

If you're a cheesecake lover, but don't want to spend hours in the kitchen baking, then the No-Bake Cheesecakes cookbook is perfect for you. With 100 delicious and easy-to-make no-bake cheesecake recipes, you'll never run out of ideas for a sweet treat.

From classic flavors like chocolate and strawberry to more unique combinations like peanut butter and jelly or blueberry lemon, there's a cheesecake recipe for every taste bud. You'll also find vegan and gluten-free options, so everyone can indulge in the creamy goodness.

In addition to traditional cheesecakes, the cookbook features recipes for cheesecake bars, cheesecake bites, and even cheesecake ice cream. There are recipes for all occasions, whether you're looking to impress guests at a dinner party or simply want to treat yourself on a lazy weekend.

Each recipe comes with step-by-step instructions and beautiful photos to guide you through the process. You'll also find helpful tips for ingredient substitutions and decorating ideas to take your cheesecake game to the next level.

So, whether you're a beginner or a seasoned baker, the No-Bake Cheesecakes cookbook has something for everyone. Get ready to indulge in the rich and creamy world of no-bake cheesecakes.

FLORAL CHEESECAKES

1. No-Bake Rose Cheesecake

Makes: 4 Servings

INGREDIENTS

FOR THE BISCUIT BASE
- 50 gm Marie Biscuits
- 20 gm Melted Butter

FOR THE CHEESECAKE MIX
- 150 gm Cream Cheese
- 75 gm Whipping Cream
- 20 gm Icing sugar
- Rose Essence
- Pink Food Color a few drops

INSTRUCTIONS

a) Grind the biscuits, add melted butter and mix until incorporated.
b) Place a 5" square cake ring on a serving plate, transfer the biscuit mix, and spread it evenly with a spoon.
c) Press it down well. Refrigerate for 5-10 minutes.
d) In a bowl, combine cream cheese, icing sugar, rose essence, and pink food color. Whip until creamy.
e) In another bowl, whip the whipping cream until soft peaks form.
f) Transfer the whipped cream in batches and fold it with the cream cheese mixture.
g) When the ingredients are well incorporated, transfer the cream cheese mixture into the prepared biscuit base.
h) Level and smooth the top.
i) Garnish with rose petals and pistachios.
j) Cover with cling film and refrigerate overnight.
k) Next day, remove the cake ring gently, slice the cheesecake and serve.

2. No-Bake Hibiscus Cheesecakes

Makes:3 Servings

INGREDIENTS

BASE:
- 6 Digestive biscuits
- ⅛ cup Melted butter
- 1 teaspoon Honey

FILLING:
- ¼ cup mascarpone Cheese
- ½ cup Whipped cream, whipped
- 1/4 cup Dried Hibiscus flowers, washed
- 7 grams Gelatin, bloomed
- ¼ cup Castor sugar

TO SERVE
- Hibiscus syrup
- Candied hibiscus flowers

INSTRUCTIONS
TO MAKE BASE:
a) Crush biscuits in a mixer and add as much butter as is needed to bind them together.
b) Add honey to it.
c) Press this into small baking tin, and refrigerate it for 30 minutes.
d) Now bloom the gelatin in cold water for 10 minutes and warm it in the microwave for a few seconds and keep it aside.

TO MAKE FILLING:
e) In a bowl add mascarpone cheese, whipped cream, dried and crushed hibiscus flowers, bloomed gelatin, and castor sugar.
f) Cream all the ingredients.
g) Pour it over the biscuit base and keep refrigerated for 3 hours.

TO ASSEMBLE:
h) Serve hibiscus cheesecake with syrup and candied flowers.

3. No-Bake Edible Flower Mini Cheesecakes

Makes: 18 mini cheesecakes

INGREDIENTS

CRUST
- 2 cups graham cracker crumbs
- 5 tablespoons Light Brown Sugar
- 8 tablespoons unsalted butter, melted

FILLING
- 16 ounces cream cheese, softened
- ⅔ cup Extra Fine Granulated Sugar
- 2 large eggs
- 1 teaspoon vanilla extract or vanilla bean paste
- ⅔ cup sour cream

GARNISHES
- A handful of edible flowers, stems removed, washed, and patted dry
- 1 egg white
- 1 teaspoon Granulated Sugar

INSTRUCTIONS

a) For the crust, stir together graham cracker crumbs, brown sugar, and melted butter. Press about 2 tablespoons of crumbs into 18 paper-lined muffin cups.

b) Beat cream cheese on medium speed until smooth, scraping down the bowl as needed. Add sugar and beat until light and fluffy.

c) Add eggs and vanilla and beat until creamy.

d) Stir in sour cream.

e) Equally divide cheesecake filling among 18 muffin cups, spooning about 2 tablespoons of filling into each.

f) Set edible flowers on a paper towel. Brush a light coating of egg wash over a flower then sprinkle lightly with sugar and repeat.
g) Arrange 1-3 flowers on top of each mini cheesecake.
h) Freeze for at least 2 hours until the cheesecakes no longer look wet, but the centers still jiggle.
i) Before plating, pop cheesecakes into the freezer for 15 minutes.
j) Remove and immediately peel away the paper liners.
k) Set on a serving dish or individual dessert plates and serve.

4. No-Bake Butterfly Pea Cheesecake

Makes: 6 servings

INGREDIENTS
- 1 teaspoon Vanilla or Almond Essence

CHEESECAKE FILLING
- 750 g Silken Tofu
- 4 g Agar Agar Powder
- 170 g Sugar-Free Erythritol
- 1.5 teaspoon Butterfly Pea Powder

CHEESECAKE BASE
- ½ cup Digestive Biscuits
- 65 mL Coconut Oil, melted

INSTRUCTIONS
a) To make the cheesecake base, crush the digestive cookies in a plastic food bag using a rolling pin.
b) Then, transfer the cookie crumbs to a bowl, tip in melted coconut oil, and mix well.
c) Transfer the cookie mixture to the cheesecake tin.
d) Press the crumbs firmly with the back of a spoon down into the base to compact them and create an even layer.
e) Then, chill it in the fridge for one hour or freeze it for 30 minutes until the cookie base has set and hardened.
f) Meanwhile, rinse and drain the silken tofu to remove the brine water.
g) Slice the tofu block into cubes, tip them into a food processor, and blitz until smooth and creamy.
h) Transfer the blended tofu into a pot and tip in the agar powder a bit at a time to avoid lumps, stirring until it's incorporated.

i) Then, stir in the sugar or erythritol sweetener for a low-sugar option, followed by the almond or vanilla essence if you're using it.
j) Bring the tofu mixture to a gentle boil and simmer it over low heat for 3 minutes to activate the agar.
k) Stir the mix while it cooks to prevent it from sticking to the bottom of the pan and burning.
l) Next, spoon one-third of the tofu cream over the cold biscuit base.
m) Tap the cake tin on the worktop to remove air bubbles and level the tofu filling with a spatula or the back of a spoon.
n) In a small cup, dissolve the butterfly pea powder in little tofu cream until you have no lumps.
o) Then, incorporate the blue pea mix into the remaining two-thirds of the tofu cream.
p) Stir well until you have a uniform blue cheesecake cream.
q) Carefully pour the blue tofu cream over the white tofu layer.
r) Again, tap the cake tin on the worktop to remove air bubbles and level the blue tofu filling with a spatula or the back of a spoon.
s) Wrap the tin with cling film and refrigerate the butterfly pea cheesecake for 2-3 hours or until the filling is set.
t) Place the tin on a tall glass, unlock or loosen the cake tin ring, and carefully slide it downward.
u) Once freed, transfer the butterfly pea cheesecake onto a serving plate, remove the cake tin base, and garnish the cake to your liking.

5. No-Bake Blueberry Lavender Cheesecake

Makes: 6 servings

INGREDIENTS
CRUST
- 110 grams gluten-free graham crackers finely crushed (about 1 cup)
- ½ teaspoon dried edible lavender buds coarsely ground
- 4 tablespoons butter melted

BLUEBERRY TOPPING
- 1½ cups blueberries
- ¼ cup water
- 3 tablespoons organic cane sugar
- ½ teaspoon lemon zest
- ¼ teaspoon vanilla extract
- pinch of salt
- ¾ teaspoon dried edible lavender buds

CHEESECAKE FILLING
- ¾ cup heavy cream chilled
- 8 ounces of cream cheese, at room temperature
- 4 ounces of goat cheese, at room temperature
- ½ cup organic cane sugar
- 2 teaspoons lemon zest
- 1 teaspoon vanilla extract
- ½ teaspoon dried edible lavender buds coarsely ground

INSTRUCTIONS
a) Put the graham crackers into a food processor. Process until they're a fine, sandy texture. Transfer to a medium bowl. Add lavender, salt, and butter. Mix well with a fork to incorporate butter into all of the crumbs. Put a round piece of parchment in

the bottom of your springform pan. Press crumbs with a spoon and hands, into the bottom and a little less than ½ up the sides. Be sure to press firmly. Place in the freezer.

b) Place 1 cup of the blueberries and the water in a food processor and blend until they're chopped into small pieces. Empty the mixture into a small saucepan. Add the sugar, lemon zest, vanilla, and salt. Bring to a simmer over medium heat, stirring continuously.

c) Add the remaining half of the blueberries. Place the lavender in a reusable tea bag or cheesecloth pouch, seal it, and add to the sauce. Reduce the heat and continue to stir as the lavender steeps. When the sauce has thickened, for about 10 minutes, remove from the heat.

d) Continue to steep the lavender for another 15 to 20 minutes. Then remove the tea bag or pouch. Let the sauce cool completely.

e) In a large bowl, whip the heavy cream with an electric mixer until soft peaks form. In a second large bowl, use the mixer to whip the cream cheese, goat cheese, sugar, lemon zest, and lavender. Once the mixture is fully combined, use a spatula to gently fold in the whipped cream.

f) Take the crust out of the freezer and pour the filling in. Smooth with a large spoon. Refrigerate for a minimum of four hours best overnight. When ready to serve, remove from refrigerator and release from springform.

g) Spoon a liberal amount of blueberry sauce on top, and cut immediately. Cheesecake will last for 4 days in the refrigerator.

6. No-Bake Jasmine Cheesecake

Makes: 6 servings

INGREDIENTS
- 1 biscuit base

FOR THE CREAM:
- 400 grams of labneh cheese
- 1 cup of yogurt
- 2 tablespoons of toasted almond flour
- 1 teaspoon of vanilla
- 1 glass of sugar

JASMIN TEA:
- 2 tablespoons jasmine tea, dry whole leaf or 4 tea bags with jasmine
- 2½ cups refrigerated milk

INSTRUCTIONS

JASMIN TEA:

a) Heat up to 1 cup of milk, remove it from the stove, and put jasmine tea in it.

b) Wait for 10 minutes and refrigerate for about 1 hour to cool.

CREAM:

c) Mix cream cheese and sugar in a mixer.

d) Add 1½ cups of cold milk and the jasmine milk you have prepared. Mix for a total of 2 minutes.

e) Add the yogurt, vanilla, and toasted almond flour and beat for another minute at low speed.

f) Pour the biscuits on the base and spread with a spoon.

g) Leave in the refrigerator overnight.

TO SERVE:

h) Take the cheesecake out of the mold and carefully place it on a serving plate.

i) Decorate with jasmine flowers and serve by slicing.

FRUIT CHEESECAKES

7. [No-Bake Raspberry Lemon Cheesecake](#)

Makes: 6

INGREDIENTS:
CRUST:
- 1 ½ Graham Crumbs
- 4 Tablespoons melted butter

LEMON CHEESECAKE FILLING:
- 16 ounces cream cheese, room temp
- ½ cup sour cream
- 1 Tablespoon milk
- 1 teaspoon vanilla extract
- 1 cup Wholesome Organic Powdered Sugar
- lemon zest
- 1 Tablespoon lemon juice

TO ASSEMBLE
- 1 cup Raspberry Sauce
- Whipped cream
- Lemon wedge
- Raspberries

INSTRUCTIONS:

TO MAKE THE CRUST:

a) In a bowl, add graham crumbs with melted butter. Mix well and set aside.

TO MAKE THE LEMON CHEESECAKE FILLING:

b) In a bowl, add cream cheese, sour cream, milk, and vanilla extract. Mix on high with a hand mixer until smooth. Add powdered sugar, lemon zest, and lemon juice and mix again. Scrape down the bowl, then add to a piping bag.

TO ASSEMBLE:

c) In a 4 ounces mason jar, add 2-3 Tablespoons of the graham crust mixture and tamp down. Then, pipe in the cheesecake mixture. Shake the jar to flatten out the cheesecake mixture.

d) Add a spoonful of raspberry sauce, and top with whipped cream, lemon wedge, and raspberry.

e) Enjoy!

8. No-Bake Lime Cheesecake

Makes: 8 servings

INGREDIENTS:
- ¾ cup graham cracker crumbs
- 1 tablespoon sugar
- 3 tablespoons butter, melted

FILLING:
- Two 8 ounces packages of cream cheese, softened
- ¾ cup sugar
- ¼ cup sour cream
- 3 teaspoons grated lime zest
- 1 tablespoon lime juice
- 1 teaspoon vanilla extract
- 2 large eggs, room temperature, lightly beaten
- Lime slices and whipped cream

INSTRUCTIONS:
a) Place the trivet insert and 1 cup water in a 6-qt. electric pressure cooker. Grease a 6-in. springform pan; place on a double thickness of heavy-duty foil.
b) Wrap securely around the pan.
c) In a small bowl, combine cracker crumbs and sugar. Stir in melted butter. Press onto the bottom and up the sides of the prepared pan. Place in freezer.
d) Meanwhile, in a large bowl, beat cream cheese and sugar until smooth. Beat in sour cream, lime zest, lime juice, and vanilla.
e) Add eggs; beat on low speed just until blended.
f) Pour into prepared pan. Cover pan with foil.
g) Fold a piece of foil lengthwise into thirds, making a sling. Use the sling to lower the pan onto the trivet.

h) Lock the lid; close the pressure-release valve.
i) Adjust to pressure-cook on high for 50 minutes. Let pressure release naturally for 10 minutes; quick-release any remaining pressure. Using a foil sling, carefully remove the springform pan. Let stand for 10 minutes.
j) Remove foil from pan. Cool cheesecake on a wire rack for 1 hour.
k) Loosen the side from the pan with a knife. Refrigerate overnight, covering when cooled. To serve, remove the rim from the springform pan.
l) Garnish with lime slices and whipped cream.

9. [No-Bake Triple Berry Cheesecake](#)

Makes: 12 servings

INGREDIENTS:
- 1-½ cups graham cracker crumbs
- ⅓ cup packed brown sugar
- ½ teaspoon ground cinnamon
- ½ cup butter, melted

FILLING:
- Two 8-ounce packages of cream cheese, softened
- ⅓ cup sugar
- 2 teaspoons lemon juice
- 2 cups heavy whipping cream

TOPPING:
- 2 cups sliced fresh strawberries
- 1 cup fresh blueberries
- 1 cup fresh raspberries
- 2 tablespoons sugar

INSTRUCTIONS:

a) In a small bowl, mix cracker crumbs, brown sugar, and cinnamon; stir in butter.

b) Press onto the bottom of an ungreased 9-inch springform pan. Refrigerate for 30 minutes.

c) In a large bowl, beat cream cheese, sugar, and lemon juice until smooth. Gradually add cream; beat until stiff peaks form. Transfer to prepared crust. Refrigerate, and cover, overnight.

d) In a bowl, gently toss berries with sugar. Let stand until juices are released from berries, 15-30 minutes.

e) With a knife, loosen the side of the cheesecake from the pan; remove the rim. Serve cheesecake with topping.

10. No-Bake Blackberry Chocolate Cheesecake Cups

Makes: 6 servings

INGREDIENTS:
- 1½ cups miniature pretzels
- 2 tablespoons plus ⅓ cup sugar, divided
- 3 tablespoons butter, melted
- 1 cup heavy whipping cream
- 8 ounces of cream cheese, softened
- ½ cup confectioners' sugar
- 1 teaspoon vanilla extract
- ½ cup white baking chips
- 1½ cups fresh blackberries
- Additional blackberries

INSTRUCTIONS:

a) Pulse pretzels in a food processor until fine crumbs form. Add 2 tablespoons granulated sugar and the melted butter; pulse just until combined. Divide the mixture among 6 half-pint canning jars or dessert dishes.

b) For the cheesecake layer, beat cream until stiff peaks form. In another bowl, beat cream cheese, confectioners' sugar, and vanilla until smooth. Fold in 1-½ cups of the whipped cream, then baking chips. Spoon over the pretzel mixture. Refrigerate, covered, until cold, about 3 hours.

c) Meanwhile, in a clean food processor, puree 1-½ cups blackberries with the remaining ⅓ cup sugar; remove to a bowl. Cover and refrigerate the berry mixture and remaining whipped cream until serving.

d) To serve, top with blackberry mixture, reserved whipped cream, and additional blackberries.

11. No-Bake Apricot cheesecake

Makes: 1 serving

INGREDIENTS:
- 17 ounces Apricot halves, drained, and juice reserved
- 1 Envelope of gelatin, Unflavored
- ⅓ cup Sugar
- 16 ounces of Cream cheese
- 1 teaspoon Vanilla extract
- 1 Pie crust, chocolate wafer

INSTRUCTIONS:
a) In a blender or food processor, puree 10 apricot halves with reserved syrup; heat to boiling.
b) Meanwhile, in a large bowl, mix unflavored gelatin with sugar; add hot liquid and stir until gelatin is completely dissolved about 5 minutes.
c) With an electric mixer, beat in cream cheese and vanilla until smooth; let stand for 10 minutes.
d) Pour into prepared crust; chill until firm. Garnish with remaining apricot halves, sliced, and, if desired, whipping cream.

12. No-Bake Strawberry Cheesecake

Makes: 1 serving

INGREDIENTS:
- 1 Graham cracker pie crust
- 8 ounces of Cream cheese, softened
- ⅓ cup Sugar
- 1 cup Sour cream
- 2 teaspoons Vanilla
- 8 ounces of Whipped topping, frozen
- Strawberries, fresh to garnish

INSTRUCTIONS:
a) Beat cheese until smooth, gradually beat in sugar.
b) Blend in sour cream and vanilla.
c) Fold in whipped topping, Blend well.
d) Spoon into crust. chill until set, at least 4 hours.
e) Garnish with fresh strawberries for garnish.

13. No-Bake blueberry cheesecake

Makes: 1 serving

INGREDIENTS:
- ½ cup Sugar
- 2 tablespoons Cornstarch
- ¾ cup Cold water
- 1 pint Fresh blueberries
- 8 ounces of cream cheese
- 3 tablespoons Confectioners' sugar
- 1 teaspoon Vanilla
- 1 graham cracker pie Crust

INSTRUCTIONS:

a) Mix sugar & cornstarch in a medium-sized saucepan. Stir in water until blended.

b) Add 1 cup of blueberries. Stir over medium heat until the mixture thickens & comes to a boil.

c) Reduce heat & simmer for 2 minutes, stirring constantly, until berries release their juices.

d) Remove from heat & stir in the remaining berries. Cool to room temperature.

e) Beat cheese, confectioners' sugar & vanilla in a bowl until well blended. Spread over the bottom of the crust. Cover with blueberry mixture.

f) Refrigerate for 2 hours or until well chilled.

14. No-Bake Apple cheesecake

Makes: 4 servings

INGREDIENTS:
- 6 tablespoons Unflavored gelatin
- 1 cup Boiling water
- 2 pounds of Cream cheese
- 2 cups Confectioners' sugar
- 1 cup Heavy cream, lightly Whipped

CRUMB BASE:
- 2 cups Graham cracker crumbs
- 2 tablespoons Sugar
- 2 Red apples, cored, sliced, and Chopped
- ½ cup Chopped walnuts

INSTRUCTIONS:

a) Grease a 12-inch springform pan and line the bottom with waxed paper. In a small bowl, dissolve gelatin in water and let it cool.

b) Beat together cream cheese and confectioners' sugar until light and fluffy. Add gelatin and beat until thoroughly mixed.

c) Fold in heavy whipped cream and turn the mixture into a prepared pan and chill. Blend graham cracker crumbs, sugar, and butter.

d) Sprinkle mixture over chilled cheesecake. Press crumbs into the surface lightly.

e) Turn cheesecake over, crumb-side down, and remove from pan. Top with chopped apples and walnuts. Generously pour caramel sauce over the top. R

15. No-Bake Mango cheesecake

Makes: 4 servings

INGREDIENTS:
- 150g Arnott's Marie biscuits
- 80g butter, melted
- 2 packages of cream cheese, at room temperature
- ½ cup caster sugar
- 300ml thickened cream, whipped
- 1 tablespoon gelatin
- ¼ cup hot water
- 4 mangoes, peeled and sliced
- 2 tablespoons lime juice
- 1 mango, peeled and chopped, to serve

INSTRUCTIONS:

a) Process biscuits in a food processor until finely crushed. Add butter and pulse to combine. Press over the base of a 20cm springform pan. Chill for 15 mins or until firm.

b) Meanwhile, use an electric mixer to beat the cream cheese and sugar in a bowl until smooth and creamy. Fold in the cream.

c) Whisk the gelatin and hot water in a small bowl until the gelatin dissolves. Stir ¼ cup of the cream cheese mixture into the gelatin mixture, then add to the remaining mixture and mix well. Pour half the cream cheese mixture over the biscuit base. Top with half the mango slices, then the remaining cream cheese mixture. Refrigerate overnight or until firm.

d) Remove the cheesecake from the fridge 15 mins before serving. To make the coulis, place the mango and lime juice in a blender and pulse until smooth.

e) Arrange the remaining sliced mango over the cheesecake and drizzle over the coulis.

16. No Bake Banana Cream Cheesecake

Makes: 4 servings

INGREDIENTS:

FOR THE PUDDING:
- 3.4 ounce Banana Cream Pudding mix
- 1 ¾ cup milk

FOR THE CRUST:
- 11-ounce box Wafers cookies
- ¾ cup unsalted butter, melted

FOR THE CHEESECAKE:
- Two 8-ounce packages of cream cheese, softened
- ½ cup granulated sugar
- 2 Tablespoons heavy whipping cream
- 1 teaspoon vanilla extract

FOR THE TOPPING:
- 12-ounce Cool Whip, thawed, divided
- 3 large bananas, sliced
- 6 Wafers, crushed, for garnish

INSTRUCTIONS

FOR THE PUDDING:

a) Prepare the pudding mixture first so that it has a few minutes to chill and thicken before assembling the cheesecake.

b) In a small bowl, whisk together the pudding mix and milk until smooth. Refrigerate for 5 minutes, until ready to assemble.

FOR THE CRUST:

c) Lightly grease the bottom of a 9-inch springform pan with baking spray. Set aside.

d) In a food processor, grind the vanilla wafers until a fine crumb.

e) Add in the melted butter and combine with a fork.

f) Pour the crust mixture into the bottom of the springform pan and press firmly to create a thick crust! Set aside.

FOR THE CHEESECAKE:

g) Beat cream cheese with sugar for 3-4 minutes until light and fluffy. Add in whipping cream and vanilla and beat an additional 2-3 minutes, scraping down the sides of the bowl as needed.

a) Pour cheesecake filling into the prepared crust.

TO ASSEMBLE:

a) Once you have poured your cheesecake filling onto your crust, add your sliced bananas to the top of the cheesecake.
b) Get your pudding mixture out of the refrigerator and pour that over the sliced bananas.
c) Top everything with 8 oz of the thawed Cool Whip.
d) Refrigerate the entire cake for at least 3 hours.
e) When ready to serve, use your 6 reserved cookies and crush them. Sprinkle over the top of the Cool Whip.

17. [No-Bake Vegan Berry cheesecake](#)

Makes: 6

INGREDIENTS:
- Four 8 ounces packages of vegan cream cheese
- 0.5 ounces of Agar Agar + 1 cup of hot water
- 3 ounces of vegan lemon jello + 1 cup of hot water
- ¼ cup of powdered sugar
- wafers
- Fresh strawberries or raspberries
- Two 3 ounces boxes of vegan strawberry jello

INSTRUCTIONS:
a) In a cup of hot water, dissolve 2 packets of Agar and 1 cup of lemon jello.
b) When the cheese is ready, beat it for about 2 minutes, or until fluffy.
c) Agar Agar and jello should be added a little at a time.
d) Mix until all lumps are gone. Add the sugar and continue to beat until everything is well blended.
e) Place vanilla wafers on the bottom of the spring form. Fill the pan with the cream cheese mixture. Refrigerate for at least 2 hours.
f) Make strawberry jello with half the amount of water.
g) Allow cooling for a few minutes.
h) Place strawberries on top of the cheese mixture that has been set. Refrigerate until the jello hardens, then pour it over the strawberries.

18. No-Bake Raspberry Cheesecake Truffles

Makes: 10

INGREDIENTS:
- 2 Tablespoons Heavy Cream
- 8 Ounces of Cream Cheese, Softened
- ½ Cup Powdered Swerve
- Pinch of Sea Salt
- 1 Teaspoon Vanilla Stevia
- 1 ½ Teaspoons Raspberry Extract
- 2-3 Drops of Natural Red Food Coloring
- ¼ Cup Coconut Oil, Melted
- 1 ½ Cups Chocolate Chips, Sugar-Free

INSTRUCTIONS:

a) To begin, use a mixer to thoroughly combine your swerve and cream cheese until creamy.
b) Combine the cream, raspberry extract, stevia, salt, and food coloring in a large mixing bowl.
c) Make confident that everything is well-combined.
d) Add in your coconut oil and blend on high until everything is thoroughly combined.
e) Don't forget to scrape down the sides of your bowl as often as you need to finish. Allow it to sit in the refrigerator for one hour. Pour the batter into a cookie scoop that is about ¼-inch in diameter, and then onto a baking sheet that has been prepared with parchment paper.
f) Freeze this mixture for an hour, and then coat it with your melted chocolate to finish it off! It should be placed in the refrigerator for another hour to firm before serving.

19. No-Bake Banana Oreo Cheesecake

Makes: 8

INGREDIENTS
- 200 g Oreos
- 60 g Unsalted butter
- 3 bananas sliced

TOPPING:
- 200 ml double cream
- 1 sachet of Vege Gel
- 400 g cream cheese
- 1 teaspoon vanilla extract
- 120 g caster sugar
- 50 g Oreos broken

GARNISH
- 50 g Oreos to decorate broken

INSTRUCTIONS

a) Line a 20cm springform cake tin with baking paper.
b) Place 200g of Oreos in 2 plastic food bags and smash with a rolling pin to form crumbs.
c) Melt the butter in a pan over gentle heat, then stir in the Oreo crumbs.
d) Pour the crumb mix into the tin and flatten down evenly.
e) Spread the banana slices over the base.
f) Whip the cream with a whisk until it forms soft peaks.
g) Make up the vege gel by sprinkling it onto 200 ml of cold water and mixing then bring to a boil in a pan.
h) Set aside to cool for 5 mins.
i) Place the cream cheese, sugar, and vanilla extract in a bowl and mix well, then mix in the cream.

j) Pour in the vege gel and beat with a large whisk until thoroughly mixed in.
k) Fold in the broken Oreos.
l) Pour the mixture onto the biscuit base and smooth it out with a spatula.
m) Cool in fridge for a minimum of 3 hours to set.
n) Once set decorate the cheesecake with broken Oreos.

20. No-Bake Passionfruit Cheesecake

Makes: 12

INGREDIENTS
FOR THE BISCUIT BASE
- 200 g Gingernut biscuits aka gingersnaps
- 100 g Butter

FOR THE CHEESECAKE FILLING
- 400 g Full-fat Philadelphia cream cheese
- 100 g Caster sugar
- 2 Gelatin leaves Platinum grade, use 3 for a firmer set
- 200 ml Double cream
- 100 g Greek yogurt
- 15 ml Lime juice
- 2 teaspoons Vanilla bean paste
- 100 ml Passionfruit puree

FOR THE PASSIONFRUIT JELLY TOPPING
- 100 ml Passionfruit puree
- 100 ml Passionfruit pulp
- 75 g Caster sugar
- 2 Gelatin leaves

INSTRUCTIONS
BISCUIT BASE
a) Process the ginger biscuits in a food processor until they resemble fine breadcrumbs.
b) Melt the butter and stir into the biscuit crumbs.
c) Spoon this mixture into the base of the baking tin and press down to level.

CHEESECAKE FILLING
a) Put 2 gelatin leaves in a bowl filled with cold water. Leave for 5-19 minutes until soft.

b) Beat the cream cheese and sugar together until smooth.
c) Add the Greek yogurt and vanilla bean paste and mix in.
d) Next, warm the passionfruit puree and lime juice together in a pan until warm.
e) Drain the gelatin sheets from the water, add to the pan, and mix until dissolved.
f) Beat the fruit juices into the cheesecake batter – quick quickly once the liquid is poured in to avoid it starting to set.
g) Add the cream and beat until thick enough for a spoon to stand up in it.
h) Spoon onto the biscuit base and level using a blunt knife. Chill for 3 hours.

PASSIONFRUIT JELLY TOPPING

a) Place the remaining 2gelatine leaves in cold water and leave to soften.
b) Put the passionfruit puree and fresh passionfruit pulp into a small pan along with the sugar and heat to around 60C/ 120F until the sugar dissolves.
c) Drain the gelatin, add to the pan and stir to dissolve.
d) Let cool to around 40C/ 80F then pour over the top of the cheesecake.
e) Return the cheesecake to the fridge for a further 3 hours.

NUT CHEESECAKES

21. No-Bake Orange and macadamia cheesecake

Makes: 4 servings

INGREDIENTS
FILLING
- 1 cup orange juice
- 1 cup caster sugar
- 4 eggs, separated
- 2 oranges, finely grated zest
- 1 ½ tablespoon gelatin
- ⅓ cup just-boiled water
- Two 8-ounce packets of cream cheese, at room temperature
- 1 cup thickened cream, whipped

ORANGE AND MACADAMIA CHEESECAKE
- ¾ cup wheatmeal biscuits, broken
- ¾ cup macadamias, lightly crushed
- ½ cup butter, melted
- ¼ teaspoon ground cinnamon
- orange segments, to serve

INSTRUCTIONS
ORANGE AND MACADAMIA CHEESECAKE
a) Lightly grease a 28cm springform pan.
b) Place biscuits and half the nuts in a food processor and process until finely crushed. Add butter and cinnamon. Process until combined.
c) Press the mixture firmly into the base of the prepared pan. Chill for 15 minutes, until firm.

MAKE FILLING;

a) combine juice, sugar, egg yolks, and zest in a heatproof bowl. Whisk over a saucepan of simmering water for 4-5 minutes until thick and frothy. Remove from heat.
b) Meanwhile, in a small jug, whisk gelatin briskly into the water with a fork until dissolved. Cool slightly.
c) In a small bowl, using an electric mixer, beat cream cheese until smooth. Gradually blend in egg and gelatin mixtures. Transfer the mixture to a large bowl. Fold cream through.
d) Whisk egg whites in a medium bowl until soft peaks form. Fold into cheese mixture.
e) Pour into prepared pan. Top with remaining macadamias. Chill for 3 hours or overnight. Serve topped with orange segments.

22. [No-Bake Almond Cheesecake](#)

Makes: 4 servings

INGREDIENTS
FOR THE FILLING:
- Three 8-ounce packages of cream cheese
- ½ cup granulated sugar
- 1 teaspoon almond extract
- 1 cup cold heavy cream, whipped

FOR THE CRUST:
- 1½ cups crushed graham crackers
- 1 cup ground almonds
- ½ cup granulated sugar
- 6 tablespoons unsalted butter, melted

TOPPINGS:
- sliced almonds, fruit, berries, chocolate, etc.

INSTRUCTIONS
a) Cream the cream cheese and sugar.
b) Using a stand mixer and a whisk attachment, whip the heavy cream until thick.
c) Mix in the almond extract and whipped heavy cream into the cream cheese mixture, and then set aside.
d) In a 9 or 10-inch springform pan, mix the ingredients for the crust. Pat down onto
e) the bottom of the pan and freeze for 15 minutes.
f) Spread the cheesecake filling out over the crust and smooth the top of the cheesecake.
g) Refrigerate for 12 hours or overnight.
h) Freeze the cheesecake for 10-15 minutes before removing it from the springform pan.

23. No-Bake chocolate hazelnut cheesecake

Makes: 10-12 servings

INGREDIENTS
- 140g unsalted butter
- 10 ounces digestive biscuit, broken up
- 500g cream cheese, softened
- 85g icing sugar
- 300ml double cream
- 1 teaspoon vanilla extract
- 15 hazelnut chocolates
- 4 tablespoons hazelnut chocolate spread
- 25g hazelnuts, roughly chopped

INSTRUCTIONS

a) Make the cheesecake base: melt the butter in a small pan over medium heat. Blitz the biscuits in a food processor to a fine crumb, add the melted butter, and pulse until well combined. Tip into a 23cm springform cake tin and press down firmly into the base. Chill while you make the filling.

b) Beat the cream cheese and icing sugar in a bowl to soften. Whisk the cream and vanilla in a separate bowl until soft peaks form, then fold them into the cream cheese. Stir through the chopped chocolates. Spoon over the biscuit base and smooth with a spatula. Cover with cling film and chill overnight.

c) Once it has set, place the chocolate hazelnut spread in a saucepan and melt over low heat for 3-4 mins until runny. allow cooling slightly before spreading it over the top of the cheesecake. Decorate with remaining chocolates and some chopped hazelnuts. Chill until ready to serve.

24. No-Bake Almond & Blueberry Cheesecake

Makes: 1 cheesecake

INGREDIENTS:

CRUST
- ½ cup grated coconut
- 1 cup toasted almonds
- 1 tablespoon coconut oil, melted
- 1 teaspoon vanilla extract

FILLING
- 2 cups cashews, soaked for 12 hours, rinsed, and drained
- 3 tablespoons lemon juice at room temperature
- ½ cup maple syrup
- ½ cup coconut oil, melted
- 8 drops of infused oil - blueberry flavor
- 2 cups fresh blueberries

INSTRUCTIONS:
a) Line a 9-inch round cake pan with parchment paper.
b) Combine the crust ingredients in a food processor and blend for 1 minute.
c) Press the crust mixture onto the bottom of the prepared cake pan.
d) Glaze the crust and put it in the freezer.
e) Blend all the ingredients for the filling in a blender until smooth.
f) Remove the frozen crust from the freezer and place it on a baking sheet. Pour the cheesecake filling on top.
g) Freeze the cheesecake 30 minutes before serving.

25. No-Bake Almond Meal Cheesecake

Makes: One 7-inch cheesecake

INGREDIENTS:

FOR THE CRUST
- 2 cups gluten-free almond meal
- ¼ teaspoon salt
- 1½ tablespoons brown sugar
- ¼ cup unsalted butter, melted

FOR THE CHEESECAKE
- 1 pound cream cheese, at room temperature
- 2 tablespoons cornstarch
- ⅔ cup granulated sugar Pinch of salt
- ½ cup sour cream, at room temperature
- 2 teaspoons gluten-free vanilla extract
- ⅛ teaspoon gluten-free almond extract
- 2 large eggs, at room temperature
- 1 cup cold water

INSTRUCTIONS:

CRUST

a) Lightly spray the bottom and sides of a springform pan with nonstick cooking spray.

b) Cut a circle of parchment paper the same size as the bottom of your springform pan. Place the parchment circle on the bottom of your pan and lightly spray with additional nonstick spray. Set aside.

c) In a small bowl, mix the almond meal, salt, and brown sugar. Add the melted butter and stir with a fork until it sticks together.

d) Pour the crust mixture into the prepared pan. Spread with your fingers and press down gently to form an even layer. Place the pan in the freezer while you make the cheesecake batter.

CHEESECAKE

e) In a medium mixing bowl, beat the cream cheese with a hand mixer on low speed, until smooth. In a small mixing bowl, combine the cornstarch, granulated sugar, and salt. Add half the sugar mixture to the cream cheese and beat until just incorporated. Scrape down the sides of your bowl with a spatula.

f) Add the remaining sugar mixture and beat until just incorporated. Add the sour cream and vanilla and almond extracts to the cream cheese mixture. Beat until it just comes together.

g) Add the eggs, one at a time, scraping down the bowl well after each addition. Do not overmix.

h) Remove the crust from the freezer. Tightly wrap the bottom of the pan with aluminum foil to help prevent leaks. Pour the cream cheese batter over the crust. Tap lightly on the countertop to remove air bubbles.

i) Pour the cold water into the inner pot of your pressure cooker. Place a trivet in the pot. Use a foil sling to carefully place the cheesecake pan on top of the trivet. Make sure the pan is not touching the water.

j) Close and lock the lid, making sure the steam release knob is in the sealing position. Cook on high pressure for 40 minutes. When finished, use the quick-release method by turning the release knob to the venting position and releasing the steam.

k) Once the float pin drops, unlock the lid and open it carefully. Gently blot the surface of the cheesecake with a paper towel to absorb any condensation.

l) Carefully remove the cheesecake and place it on a wire rack to cool.

m) Once the cheesecake is completely cooled, place it in the refrigerator for 6 to 8 hours or overnight. When ready to serve, remove the cheesecake from the refrigerator. Release the sides of the springform pan and run a thin knife between the parchment paper and the crust, and then slide carefully onto a serving plate.

VEGGIE CHEESECAKES

26. No-Bake Ube Cheesecake

Makes: 12 slices

INGREDIENTS

FILLING INGREDIENTS
- 2 cups vegan cream cheese
- 1 cup ube 250 grams
- 1 cup coconut cream
- ½ cup maple syrup
- ½ tablespoon vanilla
- ½ tablespoon cinnamon

CRUST INGREDIENTS
- 2 cups of pecans
- ¼ cup coconut sugar
- ¼ cup coconut oil
- dash of vanilla
- pinch of salt

INSTRUCTIONS

a) Start by washing and peeling your ube. Then cut it roughly into smaller pieces.

b) Place the ube in boiling water and boil for 7-10 minutes, until the yam is super soft and you can easily stick a fork into it.

c) Once the ube has cooked, mash it up using a fork or potato masher.

d) Measure out 250 grams, which is equal to about 1 cup.

e) Add the ube, cream cheese, coconut cream, maple syrup, vanilla, and cinnamon to a food processor and blend all of the ingredients until super smooth.

f) I blended mine for at least five minutes on high speed because I wanted a super smooth texture.

g) Once the cheesecake filling is creamy and smooth, set it aside.
h) To a clean food processor, add the pecans, sugar, coconut oil, vanilla, and salt. Pulse them until they are well combined.
i) Line a springform pan with parchment paper and generously grease it with coconut oil.
j) Transfer the crust filling to the pan. It may be a little soft and runny, but it's okay because will harden in the fridge.
k) Use a spoon to make sure it is evenly spread on the pan.
l) Now pour the cheesecake filling on top of the crust and use a spoon to smooth out the top and create an even layer.
m) Refrigerate the cheesecake overnight or for 6 or more hours. It will need this time to fully harden.
n) Once the cake is ready, slice it in and enjoy!

27. [No-Bake Pumpkin Pie Cheesecake](#)

Makes: 2 servings

INGREDIENTS:
FOR THE CRUST
- ¾ cup Almond Flour
- ½ cup Flaxseed Meal
- ¼ cup butter
- 1 teaspoon Pumpkin Pie Spice
- 25 drops of Liquid Stevia

FOR THE FILLING
- 6 ounces of Cream Cheese
- ⅓ cup Pumpkin Purée
- 2 tablespoons Sour Cream
- ¼ cup Heavy Cream
- 3 tablespoons Butter
- ¼ teaspoon Pumpkin Pie Spice
- 25 drops of Liquid Stevia

INSTRUCTIONS:
a) Mix all of the crust's dry ingredients thoroughly.
b) Mash together the dry ingredients with the butter and liquid stevia until a dough forms.
c) Place the dough in your mini tart pans.
d) Blitz all filling ingredients using a blender and refrigerate.
e) After about 5 hours, Slice, and top with whipped cream.

28. No-Bake Cheesecake with avocado and lime

Makes: 4 servings

INGREDIENTS

FOR THE BASE
- 8 ounces of digestives biscuits
- 3 ounces unsalted butter, melted
- Zest of ½ lime
- 1 teaspoon lime juice

FOR THE CHEESECAKE
- 10 ounces cream cheese
- 7 ounces double cream for mixing with avocado
- 1 ripe Avocado
- Juice and zest from 1 lime
- 1 cup granulated white sugar
- 3.5 ounces unsalted butter melted
- 4 mint leaves
- Some mint leaves and orange/lemon/lime blossoms for garnish

INSTRUCTIONS

BASE
a) Tip the digestive biscuits into a food processor and mix until you have crumbs.
b) Add the melted butter and lime zest and lime juice, then mix until everything is evenly coated.
c) Tip the mixture into the glasses and press into an even layer using the back of a spoon.

FILLING
d) Add all ingredients, except the melted butter, into a food processor.
e) Mix well for 3-4 minutes or until all ingredients are combined.

f) Next, slowly add the butter to the mixture while continuing to mix on low.
g) The mixture should form a slightly runny consistency, don't worry, it will thicken on its own in the fridge.
h) Pour the mixture on top of the cheesecake base. Pour right to the top of the glass then use the back of a knife to 'trim' the top giving it a perfectly smooth top.
i) Refrigerate for at least 2-3 hours before serving. Garnish with some sprigs of fresh mint, some candied limes, or citrus flowers.

29. No-Bake Gingersnap Pumpkin Cheesecake

Makes: 1 cheesecake

INGREDIENTS:
- 1 ½ cups crushed gingersnap cookies
- 1 Tablespoon melted butter
- 16 ounces of cream cheese
- ½ cup pumpkin puree
- 1 Tablespoons flour
- ¼ cup maple syrup
- ¼ cup brown sugar
- 1 teaspoon pumpkin spice
- 2 eggs

INSTRUCTIONS:

a) In a bowl, mix gingersnap and butter. Set aside.

b) In a removable bottom pan line with parchment paper. Pour crushed gingersnap mixture into the pan and with a flat bottom glass, flatten it out. Put in refrigerator to firm up.

c) In another bowl, mix cream cheese, pumpkin puree, flour, maple syrup, brown sugar, and pumpkin spice until smooth. Next, mix an egg, one at a time mixing it until just combined. Finish off with a spatula. Pour into prepared cake pan and cover with foil.

d) In the Multipot, add 1 cup of water and put the cheesecake pan into the trivet. Lower into the inner pot and close the lid. Move the pressure gauge to seal and turn on the cake function for 30 minutes.

e) Once done, release to quick pressure and open the lid for a few minutes to release the rest of the steam. Turn off the machine and close the lid.

f) Let it come down to temp naturally for an hour and remove the cheesecake. Place in refrigerator for at least 4-5 hours to chill. Enjoy!

30. [No-Bake Pumpkin Pie Cheesecake Tart](#)

Makes: 1

INGREDIENTS:

THE CRUST
- ¾ cup Almond Flour
- ½ cup Flaxseed Meal
- ¼ cup Butter
- 1 teaspoon Pumpkin Pie Spice
- 25 drops Liquid Stevia

THE FILLING
- 6 ounces of Vegan Cream Cheese
- ⅓ cup Pumpkin Puree
- 2 Tablespoons Sour Cream
- ¼ cup Vegan Heavy Cream
- 3 Tablespoons Butter
- ¼ teaspoons Pumpkin Pie Spice
- 25 drops Liquid Stevia

INSTRUCTIONS:

a) Combine all the crust's dry ingredients and stir thoroughly.
b) Mash together the dry ingredients with the butter and liquid stevia until a dough forms.
c) For your mini tart pans, roll the dough into little spheres.
d) Press the dough against the side of the tart pan until it reaches and goes up the sides.
e) Combine all the filling ingredients in a mixing bowl.
f) Blend the filling ingredients using an immersion blender.
g) Once the filling ingredients are smooth, distribute them into the crust and chill.
h) Remove from the fridge, slice, and top with whipped cream.

HERBED CHEESECAKES

31. [No-Bake Basil, lime, and strawberry cheesecake](#)

Makes: 8 servings

INGREDIENTS

BASIL, LIME, AND STRAWBERRY CHEESECAKE
- cooking-oil spray
- ½ cup scotch finger biscuits
- ½ cup butter, melted
- 3 teaspoons powdered gelatin
- ¼ cup hot water
- 1½ cup cream cheese, softened
- ½ cup caster sugar
- 1 tablespoon finely grated lime rind
- 1½ cups thickened cream
- ½ cup lime juice
- 2 tablespoons finely chopped fresh basil
- 2 tablespoons fresh baby basil leaves
- 2 tablespoon water
- ½ cup strawberry jam
- 1 tablespoon lime juice
- 8 fresh basil leaves
- 1 cup strawberries, halved

INSTRUCTIONS

a) Spray a springform pan with oil; line the base with baking paper.
b) Process biscuits until fine. Add butter; process until combined.
c) Press the mixture firmly over the base of the pan. Refrigerate for 30 minutes.
d) Sprinkle gelatin over the hot water in a small heatproof jug; stand the jug in a small saucepan of simmering water, and stir until gelatin dissolves. Cool.

e) In a medium bowl, beat cream cheese, and sugar and rind with an electric mixer until smooth. Add cream; beat until smooth.
f) Add juice, the cooled gelatin mixture, and finely chopped basil; beat until combined. Pour filling over the biscuit base. Cover; refrigerate for about 3 hours or overnight until set.
g) Just before serving, top the cheesecake with strawberries and syrup; sprinkle with basil leaves.
h) In a small saucepan, stir the water, jam, juice, and basil over low heat until the jam melts. Bring to a boil.
i) Remove from heat; stir in strawberries. Cool; discard basil.

32. No-Bake Matcha cheesecake

Makes: 8 servings

INGREDIENTS
- 1 cup butternut snap biscuits
- ½ cup melted butter
- 2 teaspoon ground ginger
- 1 cup softened cream cheese
- 1 cup thickened cream
- 1 tablespoon lemon juice
- 1 teaspoon vanilla bean paste
- 1 teaspoon matcha powder, plus 1 teaspoon extra
- 2 teaspoon gelatin
- ¼ cup just-boiled water
- 1 cup melted white chocolate

INSTRUCTIONS

a) Grease and line the base and sides of a 20cm springform pan.

b) In a food processor, pulse biscuits to fine crumbs. Add butter and ginger and mix well. Press firmly over the base of the pan. Freeze for 10 minutes.

c) In a medium bowl using an electric mixer, beat cream cheese until smooth. Beat in cream, whipped to soft peaks, lemon juice, vanilla bean paste, and 1 teaspoon of matcha powder until smooth.

d) Sprinkle gelatin over boiled water and whisk vigorously with a fork to dissolve. Beat into cream cheese mixture, then gradually add white chocolate, beating to combine.

e) Pour cream-cheese mixture into the pan, reserving ⅓ cup. Whisk extra matcha powder into the reserved mixture. Spoon large dollops over the cheesecake and gently swirl through, using a butter knife. Chill, covered, for 4 hours or overnight. Serve dusted with extra matcha powder.

33. No-Bake Sweet Basil & Lemon Cheesecake

Makes: 12 servings

INGREDIENTS
LEMON CRUST
- 2½ cups vanilla cookie crumbs ¼ cup unsalted butter, melted
- 2 tablespoons lemon zest

FILLING
- 1¼ cups heavy whipping cream, cold
- Three 8-ounce packages of cream cheese, room temperature
- ¾ cups powdered sugar
- 2 tablespoons lemon juice
- 1 cup packed basil leaves, washed and dried
- pinch of salt
- small basil leaves for garnish washed and dried

INSTRUCTIONS
LEMON CRUST
a) Add the cookies to a food processor fitted with the blade attachment and blend until you have fairly fine crumbs.
b) Add the crumbs to a large mixing bowl and mix in the melted butter and lemon zest.
c) Pour into a 9-inch springform pan and press it evenly and firmly onto the bottom surface. Place the crust in the refrigerator while you make the filling.

FILLING
d) Use an electric mixer or a stand mixer fitted with the whisk attachment, to whip the cream into stiff peaks. This will take about 2 minutes. Set aside.
e) Now add the cream cheese and powdered sugar to the food processor fitted with the blade attachment. Blend until it's

completely smooth. Add the lemon juice, vanilla, basil, and pinch of salt and blend until the basil is specks of green. Use a rubber spatula to add this to a large mixing bowl.

f) Fold the whipped cream into the cheese mixture just until it's combined.

g) Remove the crust from the refrigerator and pour the filling into it the pan. Smooth the top and cover it with plastic wrap. Refrigerate overnight.

h) Use a knife to loosen the chilled cheesecake from the rim of the springform pan, then remove the rim.

i) Garnish with small basil leaves, slice, and serve.

34. [No-Bake Mint cheesecake](#)

Makes: 4 servings

INGREDIENTS

MINT SYRUP
- 1½ cups caster sugar
- 2½ cups water
- mint leaves

CAKE CRUST
- 1 cup chocolate cookies
- ½ cup unsalted butter

CHEESECAKE FILLING
- 2 cups cream cheese
- 1 cup fresh heavy whipping cream
- ½ cup mint syrup
- 10g gelatin
- ¼ cup milk
- 1 chocolate bar

INSTRUCTIONS

a) Prepare the mint syrup: wash mint leaves and pat them dry. Mince the mint in a food processor together with half the sugar.
b) Boil the water with the remaining sugar.
c) Add the mixture of mint and sugar to the boiling water and cook for 6 minutes.
d) Let it cool down for 12 hours and filter with a fine colander
e) Bottle the syrup and keep it in the fridge
f) Prepare the cheesecake crust: use a food processor to grind up the cookies
g) Melt the butter and pour it on the biscuits, mix with a spoon.

h) Pour the cookie crumb mixture into a springform pan and press it into the bottom and sides. Chill this pie crust in the fridge for 10 minutes before filling it.
i) Prepare the filling: Pour heavy whipping cream into a bowl and whisk on high speed. Keep it in the fridge.
j) Mix in a bowl the cream cheese with mint syrup.
k) Soak the gelatin in cold water for a few minutes.
l) Warm up some milk and add the squeezed gelatin. Add this mix to the bowl with cream cheese and mint syrup.
m) Incorporate whipped cream into the batter.
n) Spread filling into crust and refrigerate for 2 hours.
o) Remove the rim of the springform pan and plate the cheesecake.
p) Garnish with chocolate chips and mint leaves.

35. No-Bake Rosemary Honey Cheesecake

Makes: 8 servings

INGREDIENTS
- 400g cream cheese
- 10 ounces double cream
- 150g honey
- ½ teaspoon vanilla bean paste
- 2 sprigs rosemary
- 200g digestive biscuits
- 50g walnuts
- 120g unsalted butter

INSTRUCTIONS

a) Finely chop the rosemary.

b) Add one-half of the rosemary plus all the butter to a pan and melt on low heat. Leave to infuse as you prepare the rest of the base.

c) Blitz or crush the digestive biscuits and walnuts to a fine powder.

d) Mix the biscuit and nut base with the melted rosemary butter to form a thick paste. Line the bottom of the springform tin with baking parchment and pour the base into the tin. Put in the fridge and leave for 15-20 minutes to set.

e) Meanwhile, whip the double cream until it forms stiff peaks, and set aside.

f) Whip the cream cheese until it's light and airy, then stir in the vanilla, the remaining rosemary, and honey. Whip again.

g) Combine the cream cheese mixture with the double cream using a spatula.

h) Pour the combined mixture on top of the set biscuit base, level off, cover with cling film, and put back into the fridge. Leave for 1 hour to set.

i) To serve, push the bottom out of the springform tin and slide the cheesecake from the base to a plate or platter.

36. [No-Bake Mint Nectarine Cheesecake Tart](#)

Makes: 12 servings

INGREDIENTS
- 1-ounce Unflavored Gelatin
- 2 cups carbonated lemon-lime soda, divided
- ½ cup sugar, divided
- 1 cup graham cracker crumbs
- ¼ cup butter, melted
- 8 ounces of Cream Cheese, softened
- 1 teaspoon lemon zest
- 1½ cups thawed Whipped Topping
- 1½ cups mixed fresh berries
- 1 nectarine, sliced
- fresh mint leaves

INSTRUCTIONS

a) Sprinkle gelatin over ½ cup soda in a small bowl. Bring the remaining soda to a boil in a saucepan.
b) Add to gelatin along with 2 tablespoons sugar; stir for 3 min. until gelatin is completely dissolved.
c) Pour into a 9-inch square pan sprayed with cooking spray.
d) Refrigerate for 45 min. or until slightly thickened, stirring occasionally.
e) Combine graham crumbs, butter, and 2 tablespoons of the remaining sugar; press onto the bottom of a 9-inch springform pan. Refrigerate until ready to use.
f) Beat cream cheese, lemon zest, and remaining sugar in a medium bowl with a mixer until blended.
g) Gently stir in whipped topping; spread over the crust.
h) Decorate the top of the tart with fruit and mint to resemble flowers.
i) Cover with a gelatin mixture.
j) Refrigerate for 3 hours or until firm. Run a knife around rim of pan to loosen tart; remove rim of pan before serving.

37. No-Bake Ginger and Coriander Cheesecake

Makes: 12 servings

INGREDIENTS:

GINGER CRUST
- 25 gingersnap biscuits
- 2 teaspoons dried coriander
- 90g unsalted butter

FILLING
- 500g full-fat cream cheese
- 300ml heavy cream
- 3.5 ounces sugar
- 1 tablespoon icing sugar
- 2 tablespoons chopped stem ginger
- 1 tablespoon syrup from the stem ginger jar
- Leaves from a 30g bunch of fresh coriander
- 1 mango
- 1 tablespoon gelatin

TOPPING
- 1 mango
- 1 tablespoon gelatin
- Juice of 1 lime

TO MAKE THE CRUST

a) Start by turning the biscuits into fine crumbs, either using a food processor or by putting them in a plastic bag and crushing them with a rolling pin, and add the dry coriander.

b) Melt the butter and add to the biscuit mixture. Combine well and then tip it into a 9" spring-form cake tin. Using the back of a spoon, press the mixture down to form an evenly packed base.

c) Transfer to the fridge to set.

TO MAKE THE FILLING

d) In a blender puree the flesh of 2 mangos. Put half in the fridge for later.
e) Dissolve the gelatin in about a third of a mug of warm water and leave it to cool.
f) Very finely chop the ginger and fresh coriander and set aside.
g) In a large mixing bowl, combine the cream cheese, sugar, and icing sugar using a spoon to mix vigorously. Then stir in the mango puree and gelatin.
h) In a separate bowl, whip the cream until soft peaks form. Stir this in gently to the cream cheese mixture. Gently fold in the ginger and fresh coriander until evenly mixed in.
i) Pour the mixture into the tin on top of the biscuit base and transfer to the fridge. Allow chilling for at least 2 hours before adding the topping.

TO MAKE THE TOPPING

j) Add the juice of one lime to the remaining mango puree.
k) Dissolve 1 teaspoon gelatin in about 3 tablespoons of warm water and add to the mango mixture, stirring well. Pour the topping over the top and spread it out evenly using a spoon.
l) Return the cake to the fridge. Leave it to chill for at least another 3 hours – but ideally overnight.
m) Carefully remove it from the tin and transfer it to a plate or cake stand.

COOKIE AND CANDY CHEESECAKES

38. No-Bake Toblerone cheesecake

Makes: 8 servings

INGREDIENTS
- ½ cup plain chocolate biscuits
- ¼ cup ground almonds
- ½ cup salted butter, melted
- 2½ cups Philadelphia cream cheese, softened
- ½ cup caster sugar
- 1 cup Toblerone chocolate, melted
- ½ cup thickened cream
- 1 cup Toblerone chocolate, extra, grated

INSTRUCTIONS

a) Process biscuits in a food processor until they resemble fine breadcrumbs. Add almonds and butter. Process a further 10 seconds to combine. Press biscuit crumbs into the base of a lightly greased 20cm springform pan. Refrigerate for 20 minutes.

b) Meanwhile, using an electric mixer, beat cream cheese and sugar until smooth. Add melted chocolate and cream. Mix till well combined.

c) Spoon the mixture over the crumb base and level the top with a spatula. Refrigerate for 3 hours or overnight. To serve, top cheesecake with grated chocolate.

39. No-Bake Cookie Crumble Cheesecake

Makes: 10 Servings

INGREDIENTS:
- 1 Envelope of plain gelatin
- ¼ cup Cold milk
- 1 cup Milk, heated to boiling
- 2 packs of Cream cheese, 8 ounces each
- ½ cup Sugar
- 1 teaspoon Vanilla extract or flavor
- ½ cup Mini-chocolate chips
- 1 Deep dish graham cracker Crust
- 1 cup of your favorite cookies, coarsely crushed

INSTRUCTIONS:
a) In a blender, sprinkle gelatin over cold milk; let stand for 2 min. Add hot milk and process at low until dissolved, about 2 min.
b) Add cream cheese, sugar, and vanilla and process until blended. Arrange chocolate in the bottom of the crust.
c) Pour in the gelatin mixture; sprinkle with crushed cookies. Chill until firm, about 2 hrs.

40. No-Bake Oreo Cheesecake

Makes: 16 servings

INGREDIENTS
- 19.1 oz package OREO Cookies, divided
- 6 tablespoons butter, melted
- Four 8 oz packages of Cream Cheese, softened
- ¾ cup sugar
- 1 teaspoon vanilla
- 8 oz tub Cool Whip Whipped Topping, thawed

INSTRUCTIONS:

a) Place about 15 of the cookies in a gallon-size Ziploc bag. Crush the cookies using a rolling pin. You should still have some nice chunks.

b) Place the remaining cookies into a food processor until they become finely crushed. Mix with butter.

c) Place the finely crushed cookies onto the bottom of a 13×9-inch pan. Press them out evenly to form the crust. Refrigerate.

d) Next, combine the cream cheese, sugar, and vanilla in a stand mixer or with a hand mixer. Mix until well blended.

e) Gently stir in whipped topping and chopped cookies. Spoon the batter over the crust and spread it out evenly. Cover.

f) Refrigerate for 4 hours or until firm.

41. No-Bake Funfetti Oreo Birthday Cake Cheesecake

Makes: 12-14

INGREDIENTS

CRUST
- 25 Golden Birthday Cake Oreos
- 2–3 tablespoons sprinkle
- ¼ cup butter, melted

FILLING
- 24 oz cream cheese, room temperature
- ½ cup sugar
- 1 teaspoon vanilla extract
- 1 cup Funfetti cake mix, toasted
- 2 tablespoons milk
- 8 oz cool whip
- 1 ½ cups Golden Birthday Cake Oreo crumbs
- 7–10 Golden Birthday Cake Oreo, chopped
- 6 tablespoons sprinkle

WHIPPED CREAM TOPPING
- ¾ cup heavy whipping cream, cold
- 6 tablespoons powdered sugar
- ½ teaspoon vanilla extract
- Golden Birthday Cake Oreo crumbs, optional
- Golden Birthday Cake Oreos, cut in half

INSTRUCTIONS

a) To make the crust, add the Oreos and sprinkles to a food processor.
b) Pulse until they form crumbs.
c) Combine the Oreo crumbs and sprinkles with the melted butter and stir together until well combined.
d) Press the crumbs into the bottom and halfway up the sides of a 9-inch springform pan. Set in the refrigerator to firm.
e) To make the filling, mix the cream cheese and sugar in a large bowl with a mixer until smooth and well combined.
f) Add the vanilla extract, cake mix, and milk and mix until well combined.
g) Fold in the Cool Whip.
h) Add the Oreo crumbs, chopped Oreos, and sprinkles, and gently stir until well combined.
i) Spread the filling evenly into the crust and smooth the top. Set in the refrigerator until firm, 4-5 hours.
j) Remove the cheesecake from the pan.
k) To make the whipped cream topping, add the heavy cream, powdered sugar, and vanilla extract to a large bowl. Whip on high speed until stiff peaks form.
l) Pipe swirls of whipped cream around the top of the cheesecake. Top with additional Oreo crumbs and Oreo halves, if desired.
m) Refrigerate until ready to serve.

42. No-Bake Coconut macaroon cheesecake

Makes: 8 servings

INGREDIENTS
- ½ cup of plain sweet biscuits
- ½ cup coconut macaroons
- ½ cup butter, melted
- 2 teaspoon gelatin
- 1 tablespoon water
- 8-ounce packet of cream cheese, softened
- ¼ cup caster sugar
- 1 cup coconut cream
- 1 teaspoon finely grated lime rind
- 1 ½ tablespoon lime juice

INSTRUCTIONS:

a) Process biscuits until fine; add butter, and process until combined. Press the mixture evenly over the base and sides of an 11cm x 34cm rectangular fluted loose-based flan tin. Place the tin on a tray and freeze while you make the filling.

b) Meanwhile, sprinkle gelatin over the water in a small heatproof jug; stand the jug in a small saucepan of simmering water. Stir until gelatin dissolves; cool for 5 minutes.

c) Beat cream cheese and caster sugar in a small bowl with an electric mixer until smooth. Add coconut cream, rind, and juice; beat until smooth. Stir in the gelatin mixture.

d) Pour mixture into crumb crust. Cover; refrigerate for about 3 hours or until set.

43. No-Bake Choc Chip Cannoli Cheesecake

Makes: 8 servings

INGREDIENTS:
- 4 ounces cannoli shells
- ½ cup sugar
- ½ cup graham cracker crumbs
- ⅓ cup butter, melted

FILLING:
- Two 8 ounces packages of cream cheese, softened
- 1 cup confectioners' sugar
- ½ teaspoon grated orange zest
- ¼ teaspoon ground cinnamon
- ¾ cup part-skim ricotta cheese
- 1 teaspoon vanilla extract
- ½ teaspoon rum extract
- ½ cup miniature semisweet chocolate chips
- Chopped pistachios, optional

INSTRUCTIONS:
a) Pulse cannoli shells in a food processor until coarse crumbs form. Add sugar, cracker crumbs, and melted butter; pulse just until combined. Press onto the bottom and upsides of a greased 9-inch. pie plate. Refrigerate until firm, about 1 hour.
b) Beat the first 4 filling ingredients until blended. Beat in ricotta cheese and extracts. Stir in chocolate chips. Spread into crust.
c) Refrigerate, covered, until set, about 4 hours. If desired, top with pistachios.

44. [No-Bake Double Chocolate Cheesecake](#)

Makes: 8 slices

INGREDIENTS:
FOR THE CRUST
- 6.1-ounce box of gluten-free chocolate cookies
- 1 tablespoon granulated sugar
- ¼ teaspoon salt
- 2 tablespoons unsalted butter, melted

FOR THE CHEESECAKE
- 1¼ cups semisweet chocolate chips
- 1 pound cream cheese, at room temperature
- ¾ cup granulated sugar
- 3 large eggs, at room temperature
- ¼ cup sour cream
- 2 teaspoons gluten-free vanilla extract
- 1½ cups water
- Confectioner's sugar, for dusting

INSTRUCTIONS:
CRUST
a) Spray a springform pan with nonstick cooking spray. Cut a parchment circle the same size as the bottom of the pan and place it inside your pan. Spray the parchment. Set aside.
b) Place the cookies in the bowl of a food processor and pulse until they resemble coarse sand. Pour the cookie crumbs into a medium bowl and add the sugar and salt. Stir to combine. Add the melted butter and stir until the mixture sticks together.
c) Gently press the crumbs evenly on the bottom of the prepared pan. Use your fingers or a flat-bottom glass to help press the crust in place. Put the crust in the freezer while you make the filling.

CHEESECAKE
d) In a medium microwave-safe bowl, melt the chocolate chips on high power, stirring every 30 seconds, until smooth and completely melted. Let cool slightly.
e) In the bowl of a stand mixer, beat the cream cheese until smooth. Add the ¾ cup granulated sugar and continue to beat. Add the eggs, one at a time, beating for 1 minute and scraping down the sides of the bowl after each addition. Beat in the sour cream and vanilla until fully incorporated.
f) With the mixer on low speed, slowly add the cooled melted chocolate. Mix in completely.
g) Pour the filling into the prepared crust. Tap the dish on the counter to remove air bubbles.
h) Place a trivet in the bottom of the inner pot of your pressure cooker and add the water.
i) Tightly wrap the bottom of the springform pan in aluminum foil. Lightly spray a piece of foil with nonstick cooking spray and place

it over the cheesecake. Using a foil sling, lower the pot onto the trivet.

j) Close and lock the lid, making sure the steam release knob is in the sealing position. Cook on high pressure for 56 minutes. When it is finished, use a quick release by turning the release knob to the venting position, releasing all the steam. When the float pin drops, unlock the lid and open it carefully. Press Cancel.

k) Using the foil sling, carefully move the cheesecake to a wire cooling rack. After 1 hour, remove the foil and run a thin knife around the edges of the cheesecake to loosen it from the pan.

l) Cover with plastic wrap and refrigerate for at least 8 hours or overnight, until fully set.

m) Cut into 8 slices and serve with a sprinkle of confectioner's sugar on top.

45. No-Bake Mocha Cheesecake

Makes: 12 Slices

INGREDIENTS

BISCUIT BASE
- 300 g digestives
- 150 g unsalted butter
- 25 g cocoa powder

CHEESECAKE FILLING
- 150 g milk chocolate
- 2 teaspoon camp coffee
- 500 g full-fat cream cheese
- 100 g icing sugar
- 1 teaspoon vanilla extract
- 300 ml double cream

DECORATION
- 100 g milk chocolate
- 150 ml double cream
- 2 tablespoons icing sugar
- 1 teaspoon camp coffee
- Sprinkles

INSTRUCTIONS
FOR THE BISCUIT BASE
a) Blitz the digestives in a food processor with the cocoa powder until it's a fine crumb.
b) Mix the biscuits in with the melted butter and press down into the bottom of an 8"/20cm deep springform tin and refrigerate whilst you make the filling!

FOR THE FILLING
c) Melt the milk chocolate carefully and leave to the side to cool slightly.
d) Using an electric stand mixer, whisk together the cream cheese, vanilla, and icing sugar until smooth.
e) Add the double cream and whisk together until it holds itself.
f) Split the mixtures into two bowls. To one-half, add the melted milk chocolate and mix it. In the other, add the camp coffee extract and mix until combined as well.
g) When mixed, dollop the mixtures onto the biscuit base randomly and swirl them together. Smooth over the top and refrigerate for 6+ hours to set, or preferably overnight.

TO DECORATE
h) Once set, remove it from the tin. Whip together the double cream, camp coffee extract, and icing sugar until thick and pipeable.
i) Drizzle over some melted milk chocolate, pipe on some of the delicious coffee whipped cream, and sprinkle on some pretty sprinkles!

46. No-Bake Peanut Butter Cheesecake Bombs

Makes: 12

INGREDIENTS:
- 6 ounces of Cream Cheese
- ⅓ cup Natural Creamy Peanut Butter
- 2 tablespoons of Xylitol
- 1 teaspoon of Vanilla Extract
- 1 pinch of 1 cup of Heavy Cream
- ⅛ tablespoons of Xanthan Gum
- 3 bars of Double Chocolate Crunch Bar, Snack Caramel

INSTRUCTIONS:

a) To make the cream cheese creamy, use a mixer set on medium speed to whip the softened cream cheese. Combine the powdered granular sugar replacement, peanut butter, and vanilla in a mixing bowl until well combined.

b) Add 1 cup of heavy cream and ¼ teaspoon of xanthan gum, and beat until the mixture is light and fluffy in texture.

c) Make three segments out of the Atkins bars by slicing them lengthwise and coarsely chopping them. Using a 2-tablespoon scoop onto wax paper that has been conveniently coated with a baking sheet, fold the ingredients into the mixture.

d) Place in the freezer until completely frozen.

BOOZY CHEESECAKES

47. No-Bake Rum eggnog cheesecake

Makes: 1 serving

INGREDIENTS:
- 1¼ cup Vanilla wafers, finely crushed
- 3 tablespoons Butter, melted
- ⅓ cup Sugar
- 1 pack of Unflavored gelatin
- 1 cup Eggnog
- 4 Egg yolks, beaten
- ¼ teaspoon Ground nutmeg
- 16 ounces Cream cheese, softened
- 2 tablespoons Rum
- 4 Egg whites
- ½ cup Sugar
- ½ cup Whipping cream
- Shaved chocolate
- Crushed vanilla wafers

INSTRUCTIONS:
a) In a small mixing bowl combine the 1¼ cups crushed wafers and melted butter; toss to thoroughly combine.
b) Press the crumb mixture into the bottom and ½ inch up sides of a 9-inch springform pan to form a firm even crust. Chill for about 1 hour or till firm. In a medium saucepan combine the ⅓ cup sugar and gelatin.
c) Stir in eggnog, egg yolks, and nutmeg. Cook over medium heat, stirring constantly, till the mixture just comes to a boil. Remove from heat. In a large mixer bowl, beat cream cheese with a mixer on medium speed for 30 seconds or till softened; gradually beat in the gelatin mixture. Stir in rum or milk.

d) Chill till partially set. In a medium mixer bowl, beat egg whites on medium speed, till soft peaks form.
e) Gradually add the remaining sugar, beating to stiff peaks. In a small bowl beat cream to soft peaks. Fold whites and whipping cream into the gelatin mixture. Turn it into a crumb-lined pan. Cover; chill till firm, 3 to 24 hours.
f) Loosen sides of cheesecake from the pan with a spatula; remove sides.
g) Sprinkle shaved chocolate or wafer crumbs around the top edge of the cheesecake.

48. No Bake Margarita Cheesecake

Makes: 8 servings

INGREDIENTS:
- 8 ounces of cream cheese, softened
- 14 ounces can sweetened condensed milk
- ¼ cup lime juice
- zest of 1 lime
- 2 tablespoons tequila
- ¼ teaspoon Cointreau, orange liquor
- 8 ounces tub of whipped topping, thawed
- 1 premade graham cracker crust

TO SERVE:
- Extra Whipped Cream and Lime Slices

INSTRUCTIONS:

a) Take the plastic cover off of premade crust and set it aside for later.

b) In a large mixing bowl combine cream cheese and sweetened condensed milk with an electric mixer until smooth. Once smooth, add lime juice, lime zest, tequila, and orange liquor, and mix until combined. Fold in whipped topping until incorporated. Pour mixture into premade crust and spread into an even layer. Cover with a plastic cover that you saved from the crust and refrigerate for at least two hours, or until set.

c) When ready to serve, add swirls of whipped cream and pieces of lime that have been dipped in sugar. Cut into slices and serve.

d) Store your margarita cheesecake leftovers in the refrigerator for up to 5 days.

49. No-Bake Pina colada cheesecake

Makes: 10 Servings

INGREDIENTS:
- 1 Coconut Crust
- 2 Envelopes of unflavored Gelatin
- Sugar
- 6 ounces of Pineapple Juice
- 3 Eggs, separated
- Three 8-ounce packs of cream Cheese softened
- ¼ cup Dark Jamaican Rum
- ¼ teaspoon Coconut extract
- 20-ounce can of Crushed Pineapple
- 1 tablespoon Cornstarch

INSTRUCTIONS:

a) Mix gelatin & ½ cup sugar in a saucepan. Add pineapple juice. Stand for 1 minute. Heat over low until gelatin dissolves, about 5 minutes. Remove from heat.

b) Add yolks, one at a time beating well after each. Cool slightly. Beat cream cheese until fluffy.

c) Blend in a gelatin mixture with rum and coconut extract.

d) Chill quickly by setting the mixture over a bowl of ice water; stir until slightly thickened.

e) Beat egg whites until foamy.

f) Gradually add ¼ cup sugar until stiff peaks form. Fold into gelatin. Turn into prepared crust. Refrigerate overnight.

g) In a saucepan, combine undrained pineapple with 2 Tablespoons of sugar and cornstarch. Cook, stirring until boils & thickens. Cool. Spoon over cheesecake.

50. No-Bake Vodka Toffee apple Cheesecake

Makes: 8-10 Servings

INGREDIENTS:
- 6 red apples
- 1 tablespoon lemon juice
- 230g Grantham Gingerbread or Gingernuts
- 60g butter, melted
- 300ml double cream
- 50g icing sugar
- 150ml Greek yogurt
- 310g light soft cheese
- 2 tablespoon Toffee Vodka
- 3.5 ounces of granulated sugar

INSTRUCTIONS:

a) Peel 4 of the apples and cut them into 1cm chunks. Put in a glass bowl with the lemon juice and microwave on full power for 3 mins. Stir well. Microwave for a further 2-3 mins until mushy with a few small lumps. Leave to cool.

b) Blitz the biscuits in a food processor until fine crumbs form. Add the butter and blitz until mixed. Line the base of a loose-bottomed 20cm tin with baking paper. Tip in the crumbs and press flat with the back of a spoon. Chill until required. Line the sides of the tin with a long strip of baking paper.

c) Whip together the cream and icing sugar until soft peaks form. Put the yogurt, soft cheese, vodka, and apple sauce in a large bowl and stir gently until evenly mixed – do not over-beat. Gently fold in the cream. Spoon over the base, level with the back of a spoon, and chill overnight.

d) Core and thinly slice the last 2 apples. Pat dry with a kitchen roll. Put a sheet of kitchen roll on a microwavable plate and arrange half the apple slices on top. Microwave at 800W for 3 mins. Turn the apple slices, pat dry with a kitchen roll, and microwave for a further 3 mins until floppy and almost dry. Set aside and repeat with the remaining apple.

e) Place a sheet of baking paper on a wire rack. Put the sugar and 4 tablespoons of water in a small pan. Heat gently without stirring, until the sugar melts. Boil for 3-4 mins until you have a honey-gold caramel. Remove from the heat, add ¼ of the dried apple, stir to coat, then lift out one by one, allowing the excess caramel to drip back into the pan. Arrange on the baking paper.

f) Repeat three more times. If the caramel thickens, heat gently for 20 secs.

g) Lift the cheesecake onto a plate and remove the baking paper. Arrange caramel apple slices on top, sprinkle over crushed ginger biscuits if you like, and serve.

BAKED CHEESECAKES

51. Strawberry Cheesecake French Toast

Makes: 4 servings

INGREDIENTS:
- ½ cup cream cheese, softened
- 2 Tablespoons powdered sugar
- 2 Tablespoons strawberry preserves
- 8 slices country white bread
- 2 eggs
- ½ cup half-and-half
- 2 Tablespoons sugar
- 4 Tablespoons butter, divided

INSTRUCTIONS:
a) Combine cream cheese and powdered sugar in a small bowl; mix well. Stir in preserves. Spread cream cheese mixture evenly over 4 slices of bread; top with remaining slices to form sandwiches.
b) Whisk together eggs, half-and-half, and sugar in a medium bowl; set aside.
c) Melt 2 tablespoons butter in a large skillet over medium heat. Dip each sandwich into the egg mixture, completely covering both sides.
d) Cook 2 sandwiches at a time for one to 2 minutes per side, or until golden.
e) Melt the remaining butter and cook the remaining sandwiches as instructed.

52. Blueberry lemon cheesecake oats

Makes: 4 servings

INGREDIENTS:
- ¼ cup non-fat Greek yogurt
- 2 tablespoons blueberry yogurt
- ¼ cup blueberries
- 1 teaspoon grated lemon zest
- 1 teaspoon honey

INSTRUCTIONS:
a) Combine the oats and milk in a 16-ounce mason jar; top with desired toppings.
b) Refrigerate overnight or up to 3 days; serve cold.

53. **Strawberry cheesecake pancakes**

Makes: 4 servings

INGREDIENTS:
- 1 cup spelt flour
- 2 tablespoons sugar-free vanilla pudding mix
- ½ teaspoon baking powder
- ½ teaspoon baking soda
- ¾ cup plain Greek yogurt
- ½ cup + 2 tablespoons 2% low-fat milk
- 1 large egg
- 2 tablespoons maple syrup
- 1 cup thinly sliced strawberries

INSTRUCTIONS:
a) Add the flour, pudding mix, baking powder, and baking soda to a bowl and whisk to combine.
b) In another bowl, whisk the yogurt, milk, egg, and maple syrup until combined.
c) Add the wet ingredients to the dry ingredients and whisk until thoroughly combined.
d) Carefully stir in the strawberries.
e) Let the batter rest for 2 to 3 minutes. This allows all of the ingredients to come together and gives the batter a better consistency.
f) Spray a non-stick skillet or griddle generously with vegetable oil and heat over medium heat.
g) Once the skillet is hot, add the batter using a ¼-cup measuring cup and pour the batter into the skillet to make the pancake. Use the measuring cup to help shape the pancake.
h) Cook until the sides appear set and bubbles form in the middle (about 2 to 3 minutes), then flip the pancake.
i) Once the pancake is cooked on that side, remove the pancake from the heat and place it on a plate.
j) Continue these steps with the rest of the batter

54. Frozen fig cheesecake

Makes: 12 slices

INGREDIENTS:
- 1 cup graham cracker crumbs
- 1 cup plus 2 tablespoons granulated sugar
- 4 tablespoons butter, melted
- 2 cups ricotta cheese, drained
- 8 ounces of cream cheese
- 1 tablespoons cornstarch
- 4 large eggs
- 2 teaspoon vanilla extract
- Pinch salt
- ⅓ cup fig jam

INSTRUCTIONS:

a) Heat the oven to 340°F (171°C). Wrap the inside of a 9-inch (23cm) springform pan with aluminum foil. Spray with nonstick cooking spray and set aside.

b) In a small bowl, combine graham cracker crumbs, 2 tablespoons of sugar, and butter. Press into the bottom of the prepared pan. Chill for 30 minutes in the refrigerator.

c) In a large mixing bowl, add ricotta cheese, cream cheese, remaining 1 cup sugar, and cornstarch. Mix well with an electric mixer at medium speed. Add eggs one at a time, beating at low speed after each addition. Add vanilla extract and salt, and beat at low speed until incorporated.

d) Remove the crust from the refrigerator. Pour batter into the crust. Gently swirl fig jam into the cheesecake for a marbled effect. Place the pan in a larger pan of hot water so the springform pan is half submerged.

e) Bake for 55 minutes to 1 hour. The cake should be set but still, have a slight jiggle. Remove from the larger pan of water and cool on a rack until it reaches room temperature.

f) Slide a butter knife around the inside edge of the pan to separate the cheesecake from the pan, and then unclamp the outside part of the pan. Chill for 1 hour, and then freeze for 4 hours. Allow sitting at room temperature for 10 to 15 minutes before slicing and serving.

g) Storage: Keep wrapped tightly in plastic wrap in the freezer for up to 1 month.

55. <u>Vegan Berry cheesecake</u>

Makes: 6

INGREDIENTS:
- 4 (8 ounces) packages of vegan cream cheese
- 0.5 ounces of Agar Agar + 1 cup of hot water
- 3 ounces of vegan lemon jello + 1 cup of hot water
- ¼ cup of powdered sugar
- wafers
- Fresh strawberries or raspberries
- 2 boxes (3 ounces each) of vegan strawberry jello

INSTRUCTIONS:
a) In a cup of hot water, dissolve 2 packets of Agar and 1 cup of lemon jello.
b) When the cheese is ready, beat it for about 2 minutes, or until fluffy. Agar Agar and jello should be added a little at a time.
c) Mix until all lumps are gone. Add the sugar and continue to beat until everything is well blended.
d) Place vanilla wafers on the bottom of the spring form. Fill the pan with the cream cheese mixture. Refrigerate for at least 2 hours.
e) Make strawberry jello with half the amount of water (1 cup for each box, a total of 2 cups from two boxes). Allow cooling for a few minutes.
f) Place strawberries on top of the cheese mixture that has been set. Refrigerate until the jello hardens, then pour it over the strawberries.

56. Mango cheesecake

Makes: 6 Servings

INGREDIENTS:

CRUST
- 7 sheets Graham crackers, crushed
- 2 tablespoons unsalted butter, melted

FILLING
- 1 pound cream cheese,
- ½ cup mango pulp, plus 1½ teaspoons
- ½ cup sugar
- 1 tablespoon curry powder
- 2 teaspoons all-purpose flour
- 2 large eggs plus 1 egg yolk

INSTRUCTIONS:
a) Fill the Instant Pot halfway with water and add the wire-metal steam rack.
b) Combine the Graham crackers and melted butter in a food processor until smooth.
c) Spread the Graham cracker mixture evenly on the bottom of the prepared pan. Freeze
d) To make the filling, whirl together the cream cheese, 12-cup mango pulp, curry powder, sugar, and flour in a blender until smooth.
e) Crack in the eggs
f) Fill the frozen crust with the filling.
g) Drizzle the remaining 112 tablespoons of mango pulp on top.
h) Place an 8-inch sheet of aluminum foil over the top of the pan and cover it with a paper towel.
i) In the Instant Pot, place the pan on the rack.
j) Preheat the oven to high pressure for 37 minutes.
k) Leave the cheesecake to cool for about an hour on the counter. Refrigerate.
l) Serve cold, and cut into wedges.

57. **Blueberry Cheesecake**

Makes: 10

INGREDIENTS:
FOR THE CRUST:
- 2 cups crushed gluten-free graham crackers ¼ cup white sugar
- 6 tablespoons unsalted butter, melted

FOR THE FILLING:
- 2 ½ (8-ounce) packages of cream cheese, softened
- ½ cup honey
- 3 large eggs
- 2 tablespoons milk
- 1 ½ teaspoon vanilla extract
- ¼ teaspoon salt

FOR THE COULIS:
- 250g blueberries (or other berries if you prefer)
- 100ml / 6 tablespoons water
- 2 tablespoons of maple syrup/agave nectar

INSTRUCTIONS:
a) Preheat the oven to 180C / 350F
b) Stir together the crust ingredients until it is well combined.
c) Pour the crust mixture into a 9-inch round springform pan and press it evenly along the butter and about 1 inch up the sides.
d) Bake the crust for 8 minutes then set aside to cool.
e) In a mixing bowl, beat the cream cheese and honey together until smooth.
f) In a separate bowl, beat together the eggs, milk, vanilla extract, and salt. Add the mixture to the cream cheese mixture and blend well.
g) Fold in the blackberries taking care not to break them up.
h) Pour the filling into the cooled crust and bake for 30 minutes or until the cheesecake is just set in the center.
i) Let the cheesecake cool then gently remove the sides of the springform pan.
j) Chill the cheesecake for at least 4 hours before serving.
k) Make the coulis by putting the berries in a saucepan with the water and syrup, and cook on medium heat for 2-3 minutes.
l) Take off the heat and allow it to cool. You can whizz it up to make smooth or leave it as it is.
m) Top the cheesecake with the coulis.

58. Cranberry orange cheesecake

Makes: 12 servings

INGREDIENTS:
- 1 cup Graham crumbs
- 2 cups Cottage cheese
- 1 pack Light cream cheese; 8oz
- ⅔ cup Sugar
- ½ cup Plain yogurt
- ¼ cup Flour; all-purpose
- 2 cups Cranberries
- ½ cup Orange juice
- 1 tablespoon Margarine; light, melted
- 2 Egg whites
- 1 Egg
- 1 tablespoon Orange rind; grated
- 1 teaspoon Vanilla
- ⅓ cup Sugar
- 2 teaspoons Cornstarch

INSTRUCTIONS:
a) Combine crust ingredients. Press over the bottom of the 9-inch springform pan.
b) Bake at 325 degrees F for 5 minutes.
c) In a food processor, blend cottage cheese until smooth. Add cream cheese and process until smooth. Add remaining filling ingredients; process until smooth. Pour into pan. Bake at 325 degrees F for 50 to 60 minutes or until almost set in the center.
d) Run a knife around the edge of the cake to Loosen it from the rim. Cool on rack. Chill.
e) Combine cranberries, orange juice, and sugar in a saucepan. Bring to a boil, stirring constantly. Then simmer for 3 minutes or until cranberries start to pop. Dissolve cornstarch in 1 tablespoons water. Add to pan, cook, and stir for 2 minutes.
f) Chill the topping, and spread it over the cake before serving.

59. **Lemond Rind cheesecake**

Makes: 10 servings

INGREDIENTS:
- 1 pound Cream Cheese
- 1½ cup Sugar; Granulated
- 2 eggs
- ½ teaspoon Cinnamon; Ground
- 1 teaspoon Lemon Rind; Grated
- ¼ cup Unbleached Flour
- ½ teaspoon Salt
- 1 x Confectioners' Sugar
- 3 tablespoons Butter

INSTRUCTIONS:
a) Preheat oven to 400 degrees Fahrenheit. Cream together the cheese, 1 tablespoon of butter, and the sugar in a large mixing basin. Do not thrash.
b) Add the eggs one at a time, beating thoroughly after each addition.
c) Combine the cinnamon, lemon rind, flour, and salt. Butter the pan with the remaining 2 tablespoons of butter, spreading it evenly with your fingers.
d) Pour the batter into the prepared pan and bake at 400 degrees for 12 minutes, then decrease to 350 degrees and bake for another 25 to 30 minutes. The knife should be free of any residue.
e) When the cake has cooled to room temperature, dust it with confectioners' sugar.

60. Upside-down pineapple cheesecakes

Makes: 4 Mini cakes

INGREDIENTS:
- 1 tablespoon Unsalted butter
- ¼ cup Graham cracker crumbs
- ¾ cup Cream cheese softened (6oz)
- ¼ cup + 1 teaspoon sugar
- ¼ teaspoon Fresh grated lemon zest
- ¼ teaspoon Vanilla
- 1 Large egg
- 1 teaspoon Cornstarch
- ½ cup Drained canned crushed
- Pineapple, reserve 1 T juice
- ½ cup Water

INSTRUCTIONS:
a) In small saucepan melt butter over moderate heat, stir in graham crumbs, and then divide the mixture among 4 paper lines ½ cup muffin tins, pressing in to form a crust.
b) Bake the crusts in the middle of a preheated 350F oven for 5 minutes, and then let cool on a rack for 5 minutes.
c) In a bowl with an electric mixer, beat together the cream cheese, ¼ cup of the sugar, the zest, and the vanilla until the mixture is combined well.
d) Add the egg, beat in until well combined, and divide the batter among the tins. Bake the cheesecakes in the middle of a preheated 350F oven for 20 minutes or until they are set, and let them cool on a rack for 10 minutes.
e) While the cheesecakes are baking, in a small bowl dissolve the cornstarch in the reserved pineapple juice. In a small saucepan simmer the crushed pineapple with the water and the remaining 1 teaspoon of sugar for 5 minutes, or until the liquid is reduced to about 2 tablespoons.
f) Stir the cornstarch mixture and stir it into the pineapple mixture.
g) Simmer the sauce, stirring, for 2 minutes, transfer it to a metal bowl set in a larger bowl of ice and cold water, and let it cool, stirring occasionally.
h) Spoon the sauce onto 2 plates and invert the cheesecakes onto the sauce, discarding the paper.

61. Tangerine cheesecake

Makes: 2 servings

INGREDIENTS:
- 1 cup Graham Crackers; Crushed
- 2 tablespoons Sugar
- 3 packs 8 ounces of Cream Cheese; Softened
- 4 Eggs
- 1 cup Sugar
- 1½ cup Sour Cream
- 2 teaspoons Vanilla
- 2 tablespoons Melted Butter
- 2 tablespoons Tangerine Juice
- 1 tablespoon Grated Tangerine Peel
- 2 tablespoons Sugar

INSTRUCTIONS:
a) Combine the first 3 ingredients thoroughly. Press into the bottom and sides of the 8 x 3 spring-form pan.
b) Bake for 5 minutes and cool; (350 degrees oven). Now, turn the oven to 250 degrees. Place 1 pkg. cream cheese and 1 egg in a large mixer bowl; beat thoroughly.
c) Repeat with remaining cheese and eggs, beating well after each addition. Gradually add sugar alternately with juice. Beat at medium speed for 10 minutes.
d) Stir in the peel. Pour into crust and bake for 25 minutes. Turn off the heat; let the cake stand in the oven for 45 minutes and then remove.
e) Now, turn the oven to 350 degrees. Thoroughly combine topping ingredients. Let stand at room temperature. Gently spread over warm cake.
f) Return to preheated 350-degree oven for 10 minutes. Partly cool on a wire rack. Refrigerate overnight, if possible.

62. <u>Walnut Cheesecake</u>

Makes: 10 servings

INGREDIENTS:
- Shortbread
- 2 cups Cottage Cheese
- ½ cup Sugar; Granulated
- 2 teaspoons Cornstarch
- ½ cup Walnuts; Chopped,
- 3 Eggs; Large, Separated
- ½ cup Sour Cream
- 1 teaspoon Lemon Peel; Grated

INSTRUCTIONS:
a) Preheat the oven to 325 degrees F.
b) Press the cottage cheese through a sieve and drain.
c) In a large mixing bowl, beat the egg yolks until light and foamy, then add the sugar slowly, continuing to beat until very light and smooth.
d) Add the cottage cheese to the egg mixture, blending well, then add the sour cream, cornstarch, lemon rind, and walnuts (if desired). Stir until all ingredients are well blended and the mixture is smooth.
e) In another large mixing bowl, beat the egg whites until they form soft peaks, then gently fold them into the batter. Pour the mixture into the prepared crust and bake for about 1 hour.
f) Cool to room temperature before serving.

63. **Macadamia & lime weed cake**

Makes: 14

INGREDIENTS
CHEESECAKE CRUST
- ½ cup Macadamia Nuts
- ½ cup Honeyville Almond Flour
- ¼ cup Cold butter
- ¼ cup NOW Erythritol
- 1 large Egg Yolk

FILLING
- 8 ounces of Cream Cheese
- ¼ cup Butter
- ¼ cup NOW Erythritol
- ¼ teaspoon Liquid Stevia
- 1-2 tablespoons Key Lime Juice
- 2 large Eggs
- Zest of 2 Limes

INSTRUCTIONS:
a) Preheat your oven to 350F. In a food processor, add ½ cup of macadamia nuts.
b) Grind the nuts into a coarse meal consistency, then add ¼ cup of NOW erythritol.
c) Pulse for a few moments and then add ½ Cup Honeyville almond flour.
d) Pulse again until all is combined.
e) Cube ¼ cup cold butter and add that into the food processor. Pulse again until the mixture starts to clump.
f) Add 1 egg yolk and pulse again until all of the dough clumps.
g) Remove the dough from the food processor and knead together with your hands.

h) Using some silicone cupcake molds (or just a regular greased cupcake tin), fill the wells about ⅛ to ¼ of the way full. This depends on how thick you like your crust. If you make the crust thin, you will be able to make more cheesecake cupcakes.
i) Bake the crust for 5-7 minutes at 350F. They shouldn't be browned when you take them out, they will look greasy and undercooked.
j) While the crust is cooking, beat together 1 block of cream cheese (8 ounces) and ¼ cup of butter.
k) Once the butter and cream cheese is combined, add the 2 eggs and mix again.
l) Add ¼ Cup NOW erythritol and ¼ teaspoon liquid stevia then mix again.
m) Finally, add the zest of about 2 key limes and the juice from 2.
n) Mix again until fully combined.
o) Once the crusts are out of the oven, let them cool for 3-5 minutes, and then pour the mixture into the molds. Fill them so they leave some space at the top because they will rise as they cook and can spill over.
p) Bake the cheesecakes for 30-35 minutes at 350F.
q) Cool the cheesecakes for 20-30 minutes and then store them in the fridge overnight.
r) Add some extra key lime zest over the top and serve!

64. Blueberry Cheesecake

Makes: 1 cheesecake

INGREDIENTS:
CRUST
- ½ cup grated coconut
- 1 cup toasted almonds
- 1 tablespoon coconut oil, melted
- 1 teaspoon vanilla extract

FILLING
- 2 cups cashews, soaked for 12 hours, rinsed, and drained
- 3 tablespoons lemon juice at room temperature
- ½ cup maple syrup
- ½ cup coconut oil, melted
- 8 drops of infused oil - blueberry flavor
- 2 cups fresh blueberries

INSTRUCTIONS:
a) Line a 9-inch round cake pan with parchment paper.
b) Combine the crust ingredients in a food processor and blend for 1 minute.
c) Press the crust mixture onto the bottom of the prepared cake pan.
d) Glaze the crust and put it in the freezer.
e) Blend all the ingredients for the filling in a blender until smooth.
f) Remove the frozen crust from the freezer and place it on a baking sheet. Pour the cheesecake filling on top.
g) Freeze the cheesecake 30 minutes before serving.

65. Gluten-Free Almond Meal Cheesecake

Makes: One 7-inch cheesecake

INGREDIENTS:
FOR THE CRUST
- 2 cups gluten-free almond meal
- ¼ teaspoon salt
- 1½ tablespoons brown sugar
- ¼ cup unsalted butter, melted

FOR THE CHEESECAKE
- 1 pound cream cheese, at room temperature
- 2 tablespoons cornstarch
- ⅔ cup granulated sugar Pinch of salt
- ½ cup sour cream, at room temperature
- 2 teaspoons gluten-free vanilla extract
- ⅛ teaspoon gluten-free almond extract
- 2 large eggs, at room temperature
- 1 cup cold water

INSTRUCTIONS:

CRUST

a) Lightly spray the bottom and sides of a 7 x 3-inch (18 x 7.6 cm) springform pan with nonstick cooking spray (the kind without flour in it).

b) Cut a circle of parchment paper the same size as the bottom of your springform pan. Place the parchment circle on the bottom of your pan and lightly spray with additional nonstick spray. Set aside.

c) In a small bowl, mix the almond meal, salt, and brown sugar. Add the melted butter and stir with a fork until it sticks together.

d) Pour the crust mixture into the prepared pan. Spread with your fingers and press down gently to form an even layer. Place the pan in the freezer while you make the cheesecake batter.

CHEESECAKE

e) In a medium mixing bowl, beat the cream cheese with a hand mixer on low speed, until smooth. In a small mixing bowl, combine the cornstarch, granulated sugar, and salt. Add half the sugar mixture to the cream cheese and beat until just incorporated. Scrape down the sides of your bowl with a spatula.

f) Add the remaining sugar mixture and beat until just incorporated. Add the sour cream and vanilla and almond extracts to the cream cheese mixture. Beat until it just comes together.

g) Add the eggs, one at a time, scraping down the bowl well after each addition. Do not overmix.

h) Remove the crust from the freezer. Tightly wrap the bottom of the pan with aluminum foil to help prevent leaks. Pour the cream cheese batter over the crust. Tap lightly on the countertop to remove air bubbles.

i) Pour the cold water into the inner pot of your pressure cooker. Place a trivet in the pot. Use a foil sling to carefully place the

cheesecake pan on top of the trivet. Make sure the pan is not touching the water.
j) Close and lock the lid, making sure the steam release knob is in the sealing position. Cook on high pressure for 40 minutes. When finished, use the quick-release method by turning the release knob to the venting position and releasing the steam.
k) Once the float pin drops, unlock the lid and open it carefully. Gently blot the surface of the cheesecake with a paper towel to absorb any condensation.
l) Carefully remove the cheesecake and place it on a wire rack to cool.
m) Once the cheesecake is completely cooled, place it in the refrigerator for 6 to 8 hours or overnight. When ready to serve, remove the cheesecake from the refrigerator. Release the sides of the springform pan and run a thin knife between the parchment paper and the crust, and then slide carefully onto a serving plate.

66. Fluffy Japanese Cheesecake

Makes: 1 cheesecake

INGREDIENTS:
- Vanilla ice cream
- Brownie mix, one box
- Hot fudge sauce

INSTRUCTIONS:
a) Preheat oven to 350 degrees.
b) Cut strips of foil to line jumbo muffin tin cups.
c) Layer strips in a crisscross manner to use as lifting handles when brownies are done.
d) Spray foil in a pan with cooking spray.
e) Prepare brownie batter as described on the package.
f) Divide batter evenly among muffin tin cups. Muffin cups will be about ¾ full.
g) Place the muffin tin on the rimmed baking sheet and bake in preheated oven for 40-50 minutes.
h) Remove from oven and cool in the pan for 5 minutes, then transfer to a cooling rack for ten additional minutes.
i) You may need to use a butter knife or icing spatula to loosen the sides of each brownie and then lift out of the muffin pan using the foil handles.
j) Serve warm brownie on a plate topped with a scoop of vanilla ice cream and hot fudge sauce.

67. Double Chocolate Fudge Cheesecake

Makes: 8 slices

INGREDIENTS:
FOR THE CRUST
- 6.1-ounce box of gluten-free chocolate cookies
- 1 tablespoon granulated sugar
- ¼ teaspoon salt
- 2 tablespoons unsalted butter, melted

FOR THE CHEESECAKE
- 1¼ cups semisweet chocolate chips
- 1 pound cream cheese, at room temperature
- ¾ cup granulated sugar
- 3 large eggs, at room temperature
- ¼ cup sour cream
- 2 teaspoons gluten-free vanilla extract
- 1½ cups water
- Confectioner's sugar, for dusting

INSTRUCTIONS:
CRUST
a) Spray a 7 x 3-inch (18 x 7.6 cm) springform pan with nonstick cooking spray. Cut a parchment circle the same size as the bottom of the pan and place it inside your pan. Spray the parchment. Set aside.
b) Place the cookies in the bowl of a food processor and pulse until they resemble coarse sand. Pour the cookie crumbs into a medium bowl and add the sugar and salt. Stir to combine. Add the melted butter and stir until the mixture sticks together.
c) Gently press the crumbs evenly on the bottom of the prepared pan. Use your fingers or a flat-bottom glass to help press the crust in place. Put the crust in the freezer while you make the filling.

CHEESECAKE

d) In a medium microwave-safe bowl, melt the chocolate chips on high power, stirring every 30 seconds, until smooth and completely melted. Let cool slightly.
e) In the bowl of a stand mixer, beat the cream cheese until smooth. Add the ¾ cup (144 g) granulated sugar and continue to beat. Add the eggs, one at a time, beating for 1 minute and scraping down the sides of the bowl after each addition. Beat in the sour cream and vanilla until fully incorporated.
f) With the mixer on low speed, slowly add the cooled melted chocolate. Mix in completely.
g) Pour the filling into the prepared crust. Tap the dish on the counter to remove air bubbles.
h) Place a trivet in the bottom of the inner pot of your pressure cooker and add the water.
i) Tightly wrap the bottom of the springform pan in aluminum foil. Lightly spray a piece of foil with nonstick cooking spray and place (sprayed side down) over the cheesecake. Using a foil sling, lower the pot onto the trivet.
j) Close and lock the lid, making sure the steam release knob is in the sealing position. Cook on high pressure for 56 minutes. When it is finished, use a quick release by turning the release knob to the venting position, releasing all the steam. When the float pin drops, unlock the lid and open it carefully. Press Cancel.
k) Using the foil sling, carefully move the cheesecake to a wire cooling rack. After 1 hour, remove the foil and run a thin knife around the edges of the cheesecake to loosen it from the pan.
l) Cover with plastic wrap and refrigerate for at least 8 hours or overnight, until fully set.
m) Cut into 8 slices and serve with a sprinkle of confectioner's sugar on top.

68. Japanese cheesecake

Makes: 1 cake

INGREDIENTS:
- 200 g white chocolate
- 150 g of crème fraîche
- 3 eggs

INSTRUCTIONS:
a) Separate the eggs and put the egg whites in the freezer.
b) Cut the chocolate into small pieces and melt them in a double boiler. Let the chocolate cool down a little.
c) Mix in the egg yolks and crème fraîche. Stir until a creamy mass has formed.
d) Take the egg white out of the freezer, beat it into the egg whites, and gently fold it into the mass.
e) Put the dough in a springform pan and bake it at 180 ° C for minutes. Then reduce the heat to 150 ° C and bake for another 15 minutes.
f) Finally, let it rest for 15 minutes in the switched-off oven.

69. Pumpkin Cheesecake

Makes: 1 cheesecake

INGREDIENTS:
- 1 ½ cups crushed gingersnap cookies
- 1 Tablespoon melted butter
- 2 blocks of cream cheese (16 ounces total) at room temp
- ½ cup pumpkin puree
- 1 Tablespoons flour
- ¼ cup maple syrup
- ¼ cup brown sugar
- 1 teaspoon pumpkin spice
- 2 eggs (room temp)

INSTRUCTIONS:
a) In a bowl, mix gingersnap and butter. Set aside.
b) In a removable bottom pan (or spring form pan) line with parchment paper. Pour crushed gingersnap mixture into the pan and with a flat bottom glass, flatten it out. Put in refrigerator to firm up.
c) In another bowl, mix cream cheese, pumpkin puree, flour, maple syrup, brown sugar, and pumpkin spice until smooth. Next, mix an egg, one at a time mixing it until just combined. Finish off with a spatula. Pour into prepared cake pan and cover with foil.
d) In the Multipot, add 1 cup of water and put the cheesecake pan into the trivet. Lower into the inner pot and close the lid. Move the pressure gauge to seal and turn on the cake function for 30 minutes.
e) Once done, release to quick pressure and open the lid for a few minutes to release the rest of the steam. Turn off the machine and close the lid.
f) Let it come down to temp naturally for an hour and remove the cheesecake. Place in refrigerator for at least 4-5 hours to chill. Enjoy!

70. [Pumpkin Patch Cheesecake](...)

Makes: 12

INGREDIENTS:
- 1 (16.6-ounce) package of orange cream-filled chocolate sandwich cookies
- 4 tablespoons butter, melted
- 3 (8-ounce) packages of cream cheese, softened
- 1-¼ cups sugar, divided
- 4 eggs
- 2 teaspoons vanilla extract, divided
- 1 (16-ounce) container of sour cream
- 5 drops of red food color
- 10 drops of yellow food color

INSTRUCTIONS:

a) Preheat oven to 350 degrees F. Place 23 cookies in a resealable plastic bag. Using a rolling pin, crush cookies then place crumbs in a medium bowl with the butter; mix well then spread mixture into the bottom of a 10-inch springform pan. Chill until ready to fill.

b) In a large bowl, with an electric beater on medium speed, beat cream cheese and 1 cup sugar until creamy. Add eggs one at a time, beating well after each addition, then add 1 teaspoon of vanilla and mix well.

c) Set aside 2 cookies for garnish then break up the remaining 8 cookies. Stir cookie pieces into cream cheese mixture then pour into crust.

d) Bake for 55 to 60 minutes, or until firm. Remove from oven and let cool for 5 minutes.

e) Meanwhile, in a medium bowl, using a spoon, stir together sour cream, the remaining sugar and vanilla, and the food color until well combined. Carefully spread the sour cream mixture over top of the cheesecake then bake for 5 more minutes.

f) Let cool then chill overnight or at least 8 hours. Decorate the pumpkin face with reserved 2 cookies.

g) Serve immediately, or cover until ready to serve

71. Pumpkin Pie Cheesecake Bowls

Makes: 4

INGREDIENTS:
- 4 ounces cream cheese, softened
- 1 cup plain Greek yogurt, plus more for topping
- 1 cup pumpkin puree
- ¼ cup maple syrup
- 1 teaspoon vanilla extract
- 2 teaspoons ground cinnamon
- 1 teaspoon ground ginger
- ½ teaspoon ground nutmeg
- Fine sea salt
- 1 cup granola
- Toasted pumpkin seeds
- Chopped pecans
- Pomegranate arils
- Cacao nibs

INSTRUCTIONS:
a) Add the cream cheese, yogurt, pumpkin puree, maple syrup, vanilla, spices, and a pinch of salt to the bowl of a food processor or blender, and process until smooth and creamy. Transfer to a bowl, cover, and chill in the refrigerator for at least 4 hours.
b) To serve, divide the granola among dessert bowls. Top with the pumpkin mixture, a dollop of Greek yogurt, pumpkin seeds, pecans, pomegranate arils, and cacao nibs.
c) Add the farro, 1¼ cups (295 ml) of water, and a generous pinch of salt to a medium saucepan. Bring to a boil, then reduce the heat to low, cover, and simmer until the farro is tender with a slight chew, about 30 minutes.
d) Combine the sugar, remaining 3 tablespoons (45 ml) water, vanilla bean and seeds, and ginger in a small saucepan over medium-high heat. Bring to a boil, whisking until the sugar

dissolves. Remove from the heat and steep for 20 minutes. Meanwhile, prepare the fruit.

e) Slice off the ends of the grapefruit. Set on a flat work surface, cut side down. Use a sharp knife to cut away the peel and white pith, following the curve of the fruit, from top to bottom. Cut between the membranes to remove the segments of the fruit. Repeat the same process to peel and segment the blood orange.

f) Remove and discard the ginger and vanilla bean from the syrup. To serve, divide the farro among bowls. Arrange the fruit around the top of the bowl, sprinkle with pomegranate arils, and then drizzle with ginger-vanilla syrup.

72. **Mini Monster Cheesecakes**

Makes: 24 mini cheesecakes

INGREDIENTS:
- 24 orange cream-filled chocolate sandwich cookies
- 3 (8-ounce) packages of cream cheese, softened
- ¼ cup butter melted 2
- teaspoons vanilla extract
- 14-ounce can of sweetened condensed milk
- 3 eggs

INSTRUCTIONS:
a) Preheat oven to 300 degrees F. Line 24 regular-sized muffin cups with paper baking cups.
b) Place a cookie in the bottom of each paper cup.
c) In a large bowl, with an electric beater on medium speed, beat cream cheese, butter, and vanilla until creamy. Slowly add sweetened condensed milk then the eggs until thoroughly mixed. Spoon batter into baking cups until almost full.
d) Bake for 25 to 30 minutes, or until set. Cool completely then refrigerate until ready to serve.

73. Individual Key Lime Cheesecakes

Makes: 6 individual cheesecakes

INGREDIENTS:
FOR THE CRUST
- 1¼ cups ground gluten-free shortbread cookies
- 1½ teaspoons brown sugar
- 2 tablespoons unsalted butter, melted Pinch of salt

FOR THE CHEESECAKE
- 8 ounces of cream cheese, at room temperature
- 1 tablespoon cornstarch
- ⅓ cup granulated sugar
- Pinch of salt
- 1 tablespoon Key lime juice
- ¼ cup sour cream, at room temperature
- 1 teaspoon gluten-free vanilla extract
- 1 tablespoon finely grated Key lime zest, plus more for garnishing
- 1 large egg, at room temperature
- 1½ cups water
- Whipped cream, for garnishing

INSTRUCTIONS:
CRUST
a) Lightly spray the insides of six 4-ounce (115 g) mason jars with nonstick cooking spray.
b) In a small bowl, mix the crushed cookies, brown sugar, butter, and salt. Divide the cookie mixture evenly among the mason jars. Gently press the cookie crust against the bottom of the glasses.

CHEESECAKE
c) In a medium mixing bowl, beat the cream cheese with a hand mixer on low speed, until smooth. In a small mixing bowl,

combine the cornstarch, granulated sugar, and salt. Add the sugar mixture to the cream cheese and beat until just incorporated. Scrape down the sides of the bowl with a spatula.

d) Add the lime juice, sour cream, vanilla, and lime zest to the cream cheese mixture. Beat until it just comes together. Add the egg; stir until just combined. Do not overmix.

e) Divide the cheesecake batter equally among the jars. Lightly tap the jars against the counter to release any large air bubbles.

f) Add the water to the bottom of the inner pot. Place a trivet inside the pot. Place the filled jars on the trivet, being careful the sides of the jars don't touch each other or the sides of the pot. You should be able to fit five around the edges and have space for one jar in the middle. Lightly place a large piece of foil over all the jars.

g) Close and lock the lid, making sure the steam release knob is in the sealing position. Cook on high pressure for 4 minutes. When the cooking time is finished, allow a natural release for 10 minutes, then move the knob to the venting position and release any remaining steam.

h) When the float pin drops, unlock the lid and open it carefully. Press Cancel.

i) Remove the foil and absorb any condensation on the surface of the cheesecakes by gently blotting them with a paper towel.

j) Allow the cheesecakes to cool inside the pot for 30 minutes, then remove them to a cooling rack and let them cool until they reach room temperature.

k) Cover the cheesecakes with plastic wrap and place them in the refrigerator for at least 6 to 8 hours, preferably overnight.

l) Serve garnished with whipped cream and additional lime zest.

74. Cardboard Box Oven Cheesecake

Makes: 4 Servings

INGREDIENTS:
- 2 (8-ounces) Packages of cream cheese
- ½ cup sugar
- 1 teaspoon vanilla
- 1 egg yolk
- 2 cans of crescent rolls
- 1 egg white

INSTRUCTIONS:
a) Mix the first 4 ingredients.
b) Open 1 can of crescent rolls. Pinch seams together and use a rolling pin to spread them out on a cookie sheet.
c) Put filling over crescent roll crust, leaving ½ inch at the edges.
d) Open the second can of crescent rolls, and pinch the seams.
e) Roll out on the table, the same size as the cookie sheet. Lay across filling.
f) Use a fork to seal the edges.
g) Beat eggs white until frothy. Brush on top.
h) Bake in a cardboard box oven for 30 minutes at 350 degrees.

75. **Low-Carb key lime cheesecakes**

Makes: 4 Servings

INGREDIENTS:
CHEESECAKE CRUST
- ½ cup Macadamia Nuts
- ½ cup Almond Flour
- ¼ cup Cold Butter
- ¼ cup Erythritol
- 1 large Egg Yolk

KEY LIME FILLING
- 6 ounces Cream Cheese
- ¼ cup butter
- ¼ cup NOW Erythritol
- ¼ teaspoon Liquid Stevia
- 1-2 tablespoons Key Lime Juice
- 2 large Eggs
- Zest of 2 Key Limes

INSTRUCTIONS:
a) Preheat your oven to 350F. In a food processor, add ½ cup of macadamia nuts.
b) Grind the nuts into a coarse meal consistency, then add ¼ cup of NOW erythritol.
c) Pulse for a few moments and then add the almond flour.
d) Pulse again until all is combined.
e) Cube ¼ cup cold butter and add that into the food processor. Pulse again until the mixture starts to clump.
f) Add 1 egg yolk and pulse again until all of the dough clumps.
g) Remove the dough from the food processor and knead it together with your hands.

h) Using some silicone cupcake molds, fill the wells about ⅛ to ¼ of the way full. This depends on how thick you like your crust. If you make the crust thin, you will be able to make more cheesecake cupcakes.
i) Bake the crust for 5-7 minutes at 350F. They shouldn't be browned when you take them out, they will look greasy and undercooked.
j) While the crust is cooking, beat together 1 block of cream cheese (8 ounces) and ¼ cup of butter.
k) Once the butter and cream cheese is combined, add the 2 eggs and mix again.
l) Add ¼ Cup NOW erythritol and ¼ teaspoon liquid stevia then mix again.
m) Finally, add the zest of about 2 key limes and the juice from 2 (this is about 2 tablespoons of juice). Mix again until fully combined.
n) Once the crusts are out of the oven, let them cool for 3-5 minutes, and then pour the mixture into the molds. Fill them so they leave some space at the top because they will rise as they cook and can spill over.
o) Bake the cheesecakes for 30-35 minutes at 350F.
p) Cool the cheesecakes for 20-30 minutes and then store them in the fridge overnight.
q) Add some extra key lime zest over the top and serve!

76. Cottage cheese Cheesecake

Makes: 8

INGREDIENTS:
FOR CRUST
- ¼ cup hard margarine, melted
- 1 cup low-fat graham cracker crumbs
- 2 tablespoons white sugar
- ¼ tablespoon cinnamon

FOR CAKE
- 2 cups low-fat cottage cheese, puréed
- 3 tablespoons all-purpose flour
- 1 teaspoon vanilla extract
- 2 eggs
- ⅔ cup white sugar

INSTRUCTIONS:
a) Get the oven ready by preheating it to 325 degrees Fahrenheit.
b) Combine melted margarine, graham cracker crumbs, sugar, and cinnamon.
c) Fill a 10-inch spring-form pan halfway with the crust mixture.
d) Mix the softened cottage cheese, milk, eggs, flour, vanilla, and sugar until well blended.
e) Pour the mixture into the pie crust.
f) Bake for 60 minutes in the oven.

77. **No-bake pumpkin crust Cheesecake**

Makes: 2 servings

INGREDIENTS:
FOR THE CRUST
- Store-bought Pumpkin Crust

FOR THE FILLING
- 6 ounces of Cream Cheese
- ⅓ cup Pumpkin Purée
- 2 tablespoons Sour Cream
- ¼ cup Heavy Cream
- 3 tablespoons Butter
- ¼ teaspoon Pumpkin Pie Spice
- 25 drops of Liquid Stevia

INSTRUCTIONS:
a) Place the dough in your mini tart pans.
b) Blitz all filling ingredients using a blender and refrigerate.
c) After about 5 hours, Slice, and top with whipped cream.

78. No bake mixed berry yuzu Cheesecake

Makes: 6

INGREDIENTS
CRUST:
- 1 ½ Graham Crumbs
- 4 tablespoons melted butter

LEMON CHEESECAKE FILLING:
- 16 ounces cream cheese, room temp
- ½ cup sour cream
- 1 Tablespoons milk
- 1 teaspoon vanilla extract
- 1 cup Wholesome Organic Powdered Sugar
- yuzu zest
- 1 Tablespoon yuzu juice

RASPBERRY SAUCE
- 2 Tablespoons Wholesome Organic Cane Sugar
- 1 Tablespoon yuzu juice
- 1 cup mixed berries
- Topping: Whipped cream, fresh lemon wedge, and raspberry

INSTRUCTIONS:
TO MAKE THE CRUST:
a) In a bowl, add graham crumbs with melted butter. Mix well and set aside.

TO MAKE THE LEMON CHEESECAKE FILLING:
b) In a bowl, add cream cheese, sour cream, milk, and vanilla extract.
c) Mix on high with a hand mixer until smooth.
d) Add powdered sugar, yuzu zest, and yuzu juice and mix again.
e) Scrape down the bowl, then add to a piping bag.

TO MAKE RASPBERRY SAUCE:
f) In a medium saucepan, add sugar, yuzu juice, and fresh raspberries.

g) Mix and cook on medium heat until raspberries release juice and the sauce thickens.
h) Remove from heat and let it cool completely.

TO ASSEMBLE:
i) In a 4 ounces mason jar, add 2-3 Tablespoons of the graham crust mixture and tamp down.
j) Then, pipe in the cheesecake mixture.
k) Shake the jar to flatten out the cheesecake mixture.
l) Add a spoonful of raspberry sauce, and top with whipped cream, lemon wedge, and raspberry. Enjoy!

79. Cheesecake Cupcakes

Makes: 12 servings

INGREDIENTS:
- 12 Gingersnap cookies
- 8 ounces of reduced-fat cream cheese
- ¼ cup sugar
- 1 teaspoon vanilla extract
- 6 ounces of fat-free vanilla Greek yogurt
- 2 teaspoons orange zest
- 2 egg whites
- 1 tablespoon all-purpose flour

INSTRUCTIONS:
a) Get the oven ready by preheating it to 350 degrees Fahrenheit. In a 12-cup muffin pan, line cupcake liners.
b) In each cupcake liner, place one gingersnap.
c) Using an electric mixer, whisk cream cheese, sugar, and vanilla until smooth.
d) In a separate bowl, whisk together the yogurt, orange zest, egg whites, and flour until barely mixed.
e) Pour half of the batter into muffin liners.
f) Bake for 20-25 minutes until almost set in the center.
g) Refrigerate for at least 1 hour after cooling to room temperature. Serve.

80. Custard Cup Cheesecake cupcakes

Makes: 16 servings

INGREDIENTS:
- 3 packs 8 oz Cream Cheese
- 1 cup Sugar
- 1 tablespoon Vanilla
- 3 Eggs
- 1 cup Sour cream
- Custard Cups

INSTRUCTIONS:
a) Leave cream cheese out to soften. Beat until smooth with sugar and vanilla. Add eggs, one at a time, beating on high. Fold in sour cream.
b) Will make more than what a 9" graham cracker crust will hold, so fill it to the brim, and then bake the remainder in custard cup(s).
c) Bake at 350F for 30-35 minutes, or until the crust is golden brown and the toothpick comes out clean.

81. <u>Cheesecake Bars</u>

Makes: 6 Servings

INGREDIENTS:

CRUST
- 1¼ cup graham crumb crackers
- ¼ cup sugar

FILLING
- 2 Cups Cream Cheese
- 4 Tablespoons milk
- 1 cup sugar
- 2 eggs
- 2 tablespoons lemon juice
- 1 teaspoon vanilla

INSTRUCTIONS:

CRUST
a) Mix and press firmly against the bottom of a 13 x 9 pan.
b) Reserve some for topping.
c) Bake for 8 minutes at 350 degrees F.

FILLING
d) Blend the ingredients and spread them on top of the baked crust.
e) Sprinkle remaining crumbs on top.
f) Bake for 20 minutes at 350 degrees F.
g) Cool and freeze well.

82. Pumpkin Cheesecake Bars

Makes: 2 dozen

INGREDIENTS:
- 16-ounces pound cake mix
- 3 eggs, divided
- 2 tablespoons margarine, melted and slightly cooled
- 4 teaspoons pumpkin pie spice, divided
- 8-ounces package cream cheese, softened
- 14-ounces can of sweetened condensed milk
- 15-ounces can pumpkin
- ½ teaspoon salt

INSTRUCTIONS:
a) In a large bowl, combine dry cake mix, one egg, margarine, and 2 teaspoons of pumpkin pie spice; mix until crumbly. Press dough into a greased 15"x10" jelly-roll pan. In a separate bowl, beat cream cheese until fluffy.
b) Beat in condensed milk, pumpkin, salt, and remaining eggs and spice. Mix well; spread over crust.
c) Bake at 350 degrees for 30 to 40 minutes.
d) Cool; refrigerate before cutting into bars.

83. <u>Frozen Chocolate Peanut Butter Cheesecake Bombs</u>

Makes: 12

INGREDIENTS:
- 6 ounces of Cream Cheese
- ⅓ cup Natural Creamy Peanut Butter
- 2 tablespoons of Xylitol
- 1 teaspoon of Vanilla Extract
- 1 pinch of 1 cup of Heavy Cream
- ⅛ tablespoons of Xanthan Gum
- 3 bars of Double Chocolate Crunch Bar, Snack Caramel

INSTRUCTIONS:
a) To make the cream cheese creamy, use a mixer set on medium speed to whip the softened cream cheese.
b) Combine the powdered granular sugar replacement, peanut butter, and vanilla in a mixing bowl until well combined.
c) Add 1 cup of heavy cream and ¼ teaspoon of xanthan gum, and beat until the mixture is light and fluffy in texture.
d) Make three segments out of the Atkins bars by slicing them lengthwise and coarsely chopping them. Using a 2-tablespoon scoop onto wax paper that has been conveniently coated with a baking sheet, fold the ingredients into the mixture.
e) Place in the freezer until completely frozen.

84. Raspberry Cheesecake Truffles

Makes: 10

INGREDIENTS:
- 2 Tablespoons Heavy Cream
- 8 Ounces of Cream Cheese, Softened
- ½ Cup Powdered Swerve
- Pinch of Sea Salt
- 1 Teaspoon Vanilla Stevia
- 1 ½ Teaspoons Raspberry Extract
- 2-3 Drops of Natural Red Food Coloring
- ¼ Cup Coconut Oil, Melted
- 1 ½ Cups Chocolate Chips, Sugar-Free

INSTRUCTIONS:
a) To begin, use a mixer to thoroughly combine your swerve and cream cheese until creamy.
b) Combine the cream, raspberry extract, stevia, salt, and food coloring in a large mixing bowl.
c) Make confident that everything is well-combined.
d) Add in your coconut oil and blend on high until everything is thoroughly combined.
e) Don't forget to scrape down the sides of your bowl as often as you need to finish. Allow it to sit in the refrigerator for one hour. Pour the batter into a cookie scoop that is about ¼-inch in diameter, and then onto a baking sheet that has been prepared with parchment paper.
f) Freeze this mixture for an hour, and then coat it with your melted chocolate to finish it off! It should be placed in the refrigerator for another hour to firm before serving.

85. Cookies & Cream Cheesecake Bites

Makes: 8

INGREDIENTS:
COOKIE BASIS:
- ½ cup almond flour
- 4 tablespoons cocoa powder
- ½ teaspoon vanilla extract
- 1 teaspoon baking powder
- 1 egg
- 1 tablespoon coconut oil or clarified butter

CREAM CHEESE FILLING:
- ½ cup almond butter
- 1 cup cream cheese
- ¼ teaspoon vanilla extract
- Pinch of vanilla bean paste

INSTRUCTIONS:
FOR THE DOUGH:
a) Preheat the oven to 180 degrees Celsius.
b) In a medium bowl, mix the almond flour, cocoa, vanilla extract, salt, and baking powder.
c) In a large mixing bowl, mix the egg and coconut oil until well combined.
d) Take out the biscuits and place them on a baking sheet lined with parchment paper.
e) Bake for 12 to 15 minutes or until crisp.

FOR THE FILLING:
f) Combine all ingredients in the bowl of a stand mixer and beat until smooth.
g) Add half of the crushed biscuits.
h) Scoop out a scoop of cheesecake filling with a spoon and place it on top of the remaining cookie crumbs.
i) Make sure the piece of cream cheese is completely covered with the biscuits by rolling it up. Put them in the freezer.

86. <u>Air Fryer Cheesecake Bites</u>

Makes: 12

INGREDIENTS:
- 200g cream cheese
- ½ cup Natvia
- 1 teaspoon vanilla extract
- ½ cup almond meal

INSTRUCTIONS:
a) Preheat the air fryer to 180ºC, for 3 minutes.
b) Cut the cream cheese into cubes and place in a bowl.
c) Add the Natvia (reserving 2 tablespoons for later) and vanilla and mix until nice and smooth. Refrigerate for 15 minutes.
d) Roll into 16 equal size balls.
e) In a small bowl, mix the almond meal with 2 tablespoons of Natvia.

87. **Pumpkin pie cheesecake Tart**

Makes: 1

INGREDIENTS:
THE CRUST
- ¾ cup Almond Flour
- ½ cup Flaxseed Meal
- ¼ cup Butter
- 1 teaspoon Pumpkin Pie Spice
- 25 drops Liquid Stevia

THE FILLING
- 6 ounces of Vegan Cream Cheese
- ⅓ cup Pumpkin Puree
- 2 Tablespoons Sour Cream
- ¼ cup Vegan Heavy Cream
- 3 Tablespoons Butter
- ¼ teaspoons Pumpkin Pie Spice
- 25 drops Liquid Stevia

INSTRUCTIONS:
a) Combine all the crust's dry ingredients and stir thoroughly.
b) Mash together the dry ingredients with the butter and liquid stevia until a dough forms.
c) For your mini tart pans, roll the dough into little spheres.
d) Press the dough against the side of the tart pan until it reaches and goes up the sides.
e) Combine all the filling ingredients in a mixing bowl.
f) Blend the filling ingredients using an immersion blender.
g) Once the filling ingredients are smooth, distribute them into the crust and chill.
h) Remove from the fridge, slice, and top with whipped cream if desired.

88. <u>Amaretto cheesecake tarts</u>

Makes: 24 servings

INGREDIENTS:
- ⅓ cup Sunflower seeds or almonds ground fine
- 8 ounces of Cream cheese
- 1 Egg
- ⅓ cup Unsweetened shredded coconut
- 2 tablespoons Honey
- 2 tablespoons Amaretto liqueur

INSTRUCTIONS:

a) Line the cups of two muffin tins with paper liners (one dozen each). Combine sunflower seeds and coconut. Place 1 teaspoon of this mixture in each liner.
b) Press down with the back of a spoon to cover the bottoms.
c) Preheat oven to 325F.
d) To make the filling, cut the cream cheese into 8 blocks and blend with egg, honey, and Amaretto in a food processor, blender, or mixing bowl till smooth and creamy.
e) Place a tablespoon of the filling in each tartlet cup and bake for 15 minutes

89. Cheesecake ice cream

Makes: 1 Pint

INGREDIENTS:
- 1 gelatin sheet
- 1 cup milk
- ½ serving Liquid Cheesecake
- 1 tablespoon sour cream
- ½ cup serving Graham Crust
- ¼ cup milk powder
- ½ teaspoon kosher salt

INSTRUCTIONS:
a) Bloom the gelatin.
b) Warm a little bit of the milk and whisk in the gelatin to dissolve.
c) Transfer the gelatin mixture to a blender, add the remaining milk, the liquid cheesecake, sour cream, graham crust, milk powder, and salt, and puree until smooth and even.
d) Pour the ice cream base through a fine-mesh sieve into your ice cream machine and freeze according to the manufacturer's instructions.

90. Cheesecake Sherbet

Makes: 8 servings

INGREDIENTS:
- 1 cup granulated sugar
- 2 cups buttermilk
- 1 teaspoon grated lemon peel
- ¼ cup lemon juice

INSTRUCTIONS:
a) Mix all ingredients until the sugar is dissolved.
b) Pour into 1-quart ice-cream freezer.
c) Freeze according to the manufacturer's instructions.

91. Cheesecake Ice Cream Recipe

Makes: 6 servings

INGREDIENTS:
- 4 ounces cream cheese at room temperature4 ounces cream cheese at room temperature
- ¼ cup water
- ¼ cup Swerve Confectioners
- 1 ½ teaspoon pure vanilla extract
- ¼ teaspoon fresh lemon juice
- 10 drops liquid stevia
- ¾ cup heavy whipping cream

INSTRUCTIONS:
a) Beat together the cream cheese, water, Swerve Confectioners, vanilla, fresh lemon juice, and liquid stevia until smooth in a large bowl.
b) Beat the heavy cream to stiff peaks in a medium bowl.
c) Beat ¼ of the whipped cream into the cream cheese mixture until smooth. Use a rubber spatula to fold in the remaining whipped cream ¼ at a time.
d) Gently pour the mixture into a 9-inch loaf pan, lay a piece of plastic wrap directly on top, and freeze until stiffened enough to scoop, at least 4 hours or up to 2 weeks.

92. <u>Blueberry Cheesecake Ice Cream</u>

Makes: 12 Servings

INGREDIENTS:
- 12 oz cream cheese, room temperature
- ½ tablespoons salt
- 1 cup unsweetened almond milk, room temperature
- ¼ cup mascarpone, room temperature
- 2 tablespoons vanilla
- 1 tablespoon lemon extract or juice
- ¼ cup sour cream, room temperature
- 1 cup Swerve sweetener
- 1 cup blueberries

INSTRUCTIONS
a) Prep and assemble your ingredients. If you're model recommends, pre-freeze the ice cream machine mixing bowl for at least 24 hours. Cream cheese, mascarpone, almond milk, and sour cream should all be at room temperature.
b) In a mixer with a paddle attachment, mix cream cheese until smooth. Scraping down the bowl periodically
c) Add sugar and salt while the mixer is running, and blend until the ingredients are combined and smooth. Add mascarpone, and blend until combined and the mixture is smooth.
d) Slowly add milk, vanilla, lemon, and sour cream.
e) Pour mixture into bowl and chill in the refrigerator for at least 2 hours or overnight. It must be well chilled.
f) Pulse chop blueberries in a food processor, or rough chop with a knife. A mixture that is partly chunky and partly smooshed is perfect. Chill blueberries in the refrigerator for at least 2 hours or overnight.
g) Follow your manufacturer's instructions for making ice cream. The model we used comes with a frozen bowl attachment that

is pre-frozen for 24 hours in the freezer. No salt and ice are needed.

h) Set up your ice cream maker according to the manufacturer's instructions and turn it on. Pour the mixture into the frozen freezer bowl and mix until it starts to thicken about 10 to 15 minutes.

i) Add blueberries and continue mixing for another 5 to 10 minutes until the ice cream starts to freeze and has a soft creamy texture. Transfer the ice cream to an airtight container and freeze for a few more until it is to your desired consistency.

j) When you're ready to eat allow the ice cream to soften on the counter (if needed), scoop it up, and enjoy!

93. Apple–Cheese Ice Cream

Makes: 6

INGREDIENTS:
- 5 cooking apples, peeled and cored
- 2 cups cottage cheese, divided
- 1 cup half–and–half, divided
- ½ cup apple butter, divided
- ½ cup granulated sugar, divided
- ½ teaspoon ground cinnamon
- ¼ teaspoon ground cloves
- 2 eggs

INSTRUCTIONS:
a) Chop apples into ¼-inch dice; set aside. In a blender or food processor, combine 1 cup cottage cheese, ½ cup half–and–half, ¼ cup apple butter, ¼ cup sugar, cinnamon, cloves, and one egg.
b) Blend until smooth. Pour into a large bowl.
c) Repeat with remaining cottage cheese, half and half, apple butter, and egg. Combine with the previously pureed mixture. Stir in chopped apples.
d) Pour into ice cream canister. Freeze in the ice cream maker according to the manufacturer's instructions.

94. Cherry Cheesecake Ice Cream

Makes: 1½ quarts

INGREDIENTS:
- 3 ounces cream cheese, softened
- 1 (14-ounce) can of sweetened condensed milk
- 2 cups half–and–half
- 2 cups whipping cream
- 1 tablespoon vanilla extract
- ½ teaspoon almond extract
- 10 ounces maraschino cherries, drained and chopped

INSTRUCTIONS:
a) In a large mixer bowl, beat cream cheese until fluffy.
b) Gradually add sweetened condensed milk until smooth.
c) Add remaining ingredients; mix well.
d) Pour into an ice cream freezer container, and freeze according to the manufacturer's directions.

95. Smoked salmon Cheesecake

Makes: 1 Serving

INGREDIENTS:
- 12 ounces Cream cheese, softened
- ½ pounds Smoked salmon or Lox
- 3 Eggs
- ½ Shallot, minced
- 2 tablespoons Heavy cream
- 1½ teaspoon Lemon juice
- pinch Salt
- pinch White pepper
- 2 tablespoons Granulated sugar
- ½ cup Plain yogurt
- ¼ cup Sour cream
- 1 tablespoon Lemon juice
- ¼ cup Minced chives
- Diced red and yellow peppers

INSTRUCTIONS:
a) In a mixer bowl, whip cheese until very soft. In a food processor, purée salmon to paste; add eggs one at a time and the shallot.
b) Place salmon mixture in bowl; mix in cream, lemon juice, salt, pepper, and sugar; blend well. Fold into whipped cream cheese.
c) Pour into a buttered 7- or 8-inch spring form pan. Place filled pan in larger baking pan; surround smaller pan with 1 inch of hot water. Bake for 25 to 30 minutes.
d) Meanwhile, make the sauce.

96. Chicken-chili cheesecake

Makes: 8 servings

INGREDIENTS:
- 1⅓ cup Finely crushed tortilla chips
- ¼ cup Butter or margarine, melted
- 3(8 ounces each) Packages cream cheese, softened
- 4 Eggs
- 1 teaspoon Chili powder
- 1 teaspoon Worcestershire sauce
- ¼ teaspoon Salt
- 3 tablespoons Minced green onions
- 1½ cups Finely shredded cooked chicken
- 2 (4 ounces each) cans of Chopped green chilies, drained
- 1½ cup Shredded Monterey Jack Cheese
- 16 ounces Sour cream
- 1 teaspoon Seasoned salt
- Garnish: minced green onions
- Picante sauce

INSTRUCTIONS:
a) Combine the tortilla chips and butter. Press on the bottom and 1 inch up the sides of a 9-inch springform pan.
b) Set aside Beat the cream cheese with an electric mixer at high speed until light and fluffy. Add the eggs, one at a time, beating well after each addition. Stir in the chili powder, Worcestershire sauce, salt, and minced green onions.
c) Pour half of the cream cheese mixture into the prepared pan. Sprinkle with the chicken, chiles, and Monterey Jack cheese. Carefully pour the remaining cream cheese mixture on top.
d) Bake at 350 F for 10 minutes; reduce the heat to 300F, and bake for an additional hour or until set. Cool completely on a wire rack.
e) Combine the sour cream and seasoned salt. Spread evenly over the top of the cheesecake. Cover and chill for at least 8 hours. Garnish, if desired, and serve with Picante sauce.

97. Crab meat cheesecakes with crab

Makes: 4 Servings

INGREDIENTS:
- 2½ pounds Cooked crab; picked over, shells reserved
- 4 cups Water
- 1 cup Dry white wine
- 1 Onion; chopped
- 2 Carrots; chopped
- 1 Clove garlic; minced
- 2 tablespoons Tomato paste
- 1 Bouquet garnish; 3 parsley sprigs, 3 thyme sprigs, 1 bay leaf & 10 peppercorns
- ½ cup Whipping cream
- 6 ounces of Cream cheese; at room temperature
- 2 Eggs
- ½ Shallot; minced
- 1 tablespoon Chopped tomatoes; seeded
- 1 small Clove of garlic; minced
- 1½ teaspoon Fresh dill; minced
- 1½ teaspoon Fresh lemon juice
- Cayenne pepper powder; to taste
- ½ cup Chilled unsalted butter; l stick
- Caviar; optional

INSTRUCTIONS:
FOR THE SAUCE
a) Preheat the oven to 350 degrees. Crack the crab and remove the meat from the shells. Cover and chill the meat until ready to use.
b) Place the crab shells in a roasting pan and roast until aromatic. About 20 minutes. Transfer the shells to a heavy, large saucepan.
c) Mix in the water, wine, onion, carrots, garlic, tomato paste, and bouquet garnish and bring to a boil. Reduce heat and simmer

until the liquid is reduced to ½ cup, stirring occasionally about 1½ hours. Strain.
d) Add the cream to the cooking liquid and simmer until reduced to ¾ cup, stirring occasionally about 10 minutes.
e) Cover and chill.

FOR THE CHEESECAKES

f) Butter four ⅔ cup souffle dishes. Using an electric mixer, beat the cream cheese in a medium bowl until fluffy. Beat in the eggs. Mix in the shallots, tomato, garlic, dill, and lemon juice. Stir in the crab meat. Season to taste with salt, pepper, and cayenne.
g) Divide the mixture between the dishes. Bake until the centers are set, about 30 minutes. Cool slightly.

TO FINISH

h) Run a sharp knife around the sides of the cups to loosen the cheesecakes. Invert 1 onto each plate. Bring the sauce to a simmer.
i) Gradually add the butter and whisk until melted. Season to taste with salt, pepper, and cayenne. Spoon the sauce over the cheesecakes. Garnish with caviar if desired.

98. Daiquiri cheesecake

Makes: 12 servings

INGREDIENTS:
- 1½ package Graham crackers, crushed
- 6 Butter, melted
- 24 ounces Cream cheese, softened
- 5 Jumbo eggs, separated
- ⅔ cup Sugar
- 2 Envelopes gelatin
- ½ cup Light rum
- ⅓ cup Sugar
- ⅔ cup Fresh lime juice
- 1½ teaspoon Freshly grated lime peel
- 1½ teaspoon Freshly grated lemon peel
- 1-pint Whipping cream
- ½ cup Powdered sugar

INSTRUCTIONS:
a) Mix crust ingredients and pat into the bottom of the springform pan. Bake at 350~F for 10 minutes. Soften gelatin in a small saucepan with ¾ cup water.
b) Stir egg yolks into sugar. Add to gelatin mixture with lime juice, rum, and rinds and cook over med. heat. stirring constantly until the mixture thickens and bubbles. Cool.
c) Beat cheese in a large bowl until light and fluffy. Slowly add the gelatin mixture and blend well.
d) Beat egg whites until soft peaks form. Add powdered sugar and continue beating until stiff peaks form. Fold into cheese mixture.
e) Whip cream and fold into cheese mixture.
f) Pour into crust and refrigerated for several hours or overnight.

99. Pina colada cheesecake

Makes: 1 Serving

INGREDIENTS:
- Coconut Crust
- 2 Envelopes of unflavored Gelatin
- Sugar
- 1 can (6 ounces) Pineapple Juice
- 3 Eggs, separated
- 3 Packs (8 ounces each) of cream Cheese, softened
- ¼ cup Dark Jamaican Rum
- ¼ teaspoon Coconut extract
- 1 can (20 ounces) Crushed Pineapple
- 1 tablespoon Cornstarch

INSTRUCTIONS:
a) Prepare Coconut Crust (see below). Mix gelatin & ½ cup sugar in a saucepan. Add pineapple juice. Stand for 1 minute. Heat over low until gelatin dissolves (5 minutes). Remove from heat.
b) Add yolks, one at a time beating well after each. Cool slightly. Beat cream cheese until fluffy.
c) Blend in a gelatin mixture with rum and coconut extract.
d) Chill quickly by setting the mixture over a bowl of ice water; stir until slightly thickened. Beat egg whites until foamy.
e) Gradually add ¼ cup sugar until stiff peaks form. Fold into gelatin. Turn into prepared crust. Refrigerate overnight.
f) In a saucepan, combine undrained pineapple with 2 Tablespoons of sugar and cornstarch. Cook, stirring until boils & thickens. Cool. Spoon over cheesecake. Serves 8 to 10.
g) Coconut Crust Mix 1½ cups vanilla wafer crumbs with 1 cup flaked coconut. Stir in ⅓ cup melted butter. Press in the bottom & sides of the 8 or 9-inch springform pan. Chill until ready to use.

100. Kahlua and cream cheesecake

Makes: 1 Serving

INGREDIENTS:
- 2 cups hard chocolate Cookie Crumbs, crumbled
- ½ cup Butter
- 3 tablespoons Sugar
- 3 (8 ounces) packages of cream cheese, Softened
- 2 cups Sugar
- 3 Eggs
- ½ cup Kahlua
- 1 teaspoon Vanilla
- 1 cup Sour cream

GLAZE
- 1 cup Confectioners' sugar
- ¾ cup Sour cream
- 3 tablespoons Kahlua
- Whipped cream for garnish

INSTRUCTIONS:
CRUST
a) Mix the crust mixture and press into a springform pan.
b) Cook for 5 minutes at 350 degrees. Let cool.

FILLING:
c) Mix one step at a time with an electric mixer. Pour into pie crust. Bake for 55 to 60 minutes at 350 degrees. Leave in the oven for 1 hour with the oven door open.
d) Remove and refrigerate until cool. Prepare glaze. Make sure consistency can be poured easily.
e) Spread on top and refrigerate for 6 hours. Serve with whipped cream.

CONCLUSION

We hope you've enjoyed exploring the world of no-bake cheesecakes with us. From classic flavors to unique combinations, we've provided you with 100 delicious and easy-to-make recipes to satisfy your sweet tooth.

Remember, no-bake cheesecakes are a versatile dessert that can be enjoyed at any time of the year. Whether you're celebrating a special occasion or simply want to treat yourself, these cheesecake recipes are sure to impress.

We encourage you to experiment with different flavor combinations and decorating techniques to make these cheesecakes your own. And most importantly, have fun in the kitchen!

Thank you for joining us on this sweet journey. We hope the No-Bake Cheesecakes cookbook has inspired you to create new and lasting memories with family and friends over a slice of delicious cheesecake..

www.ingramcontent.com/pod-product-compliance
Lightning Source LLC
Chambersburg PA
CBHW070654120526
44590CB00013BA/951